The Gifted Pastor

For Jen and Pat,

In gratitude for
our friendship, and
for the blessings
you have given to me.

In Christ,
K. Carter   10/01

The
Gifted
Pastor

Finding and Using
Your Spiritual Gifts

Kenneth H. Carter, Jr.

Abingdon Press / Nashville

THE GIFTED PASTOR
FINDING AND USING YOUR SPIRITUAL GIFTS

Copyright © 2001 by Abingdon Press

This book is printed on recycled, acid-free, elemental-chlorine–free paper.

Libary of Congress Cataloging-in-Publication Data

Carter, Kenneth H.
    The gifted pastor : finding and using your spiritual gifts / Kenneth H. Carter, Jr.
        p. cm.
    Includes bibliographical references.
    ISBN 0-687-09091-1 (alk. paper)
    1. Gifts, Spiritual. 2. Pastoral theology. I. Title.

    BT767.3 .C39 2001
    253—DC21

                                                                2001022797

Scripture quotations, unless otherwise indicated, are from the *New Revised Standard Version of the Bible,* copyright © 1989, by the Division of Christian Education of the National Council of the Churches of Christ in the United States of America. Used by permission. All rights reserved.

Scripture quotations identified as *Message* are from *THE MESSAGE*. Copyright © Eugene H. Peterson, 1993, 1994, 1995. Used by permission of NavPress Publishing Group.

Scripture quotations noted NIV are taken from the HOLY BIBLE: NEW INTERNATIONAL VERSION®. Copyright © 1973, 1978, 1984 by the International Bible Society. Used by permission of Zondervan Publishing House. All rights reserved.

Scripture quotations marked RSV are taken from the *Revised Standard Version of the Bible,* copyright 1946, 1952, 1971 by the Division of Christian Education of the National Council of the Churches of Christ in the United States of America. Used by permission. All rights reserved.

Selection from "Wesley's Covenant Service" is from *The United Methodist Book of Worship* © 1992 by The United Methodist Publishing House. Used by permission.

Permission to use hymn by Brian Wren, "Great God, Your Love Has Called Us Here" is granted by Hope Publishing Company, Carol Stream, Ill.

01 02 03 04 05 06 07 08 09 10—10 9 8 7 6 5 4 3 2 1

MANUFACTURED IN THE UNITED STATES OF AMERICA

To three wonderfully gifted congregations:

Christ United Methodist Church,
Greensboro, North Carolina

Saint Timothy's United Methodist Church,
Greensboro, North Carolina

Mount Tabor United Methodist Church,
Winston-Salem, North Carolina

1 Corinthians 1:4-8

Contents

Acknowledgments

I owe a debt of gratitude to a number of people among whom I have served during the last few years. I am grateful to three congregations in particular: Christ United Methodist Church, Greensboro, North Carolina (1988–1994); Saint Timothy's United Methodist Church, Greensboro, North Carolina (1994–1997); and Mount Tabor United Methodist Church, Winston-Salem, North Carolina (1997–). The teaching sermons were shared in one form or another with these three congregations. The vision for communities of men and women with a variety of spiritual gifts has arisen from these three very different churches.

I am also grateful to the following who helped shape this material in one way or another: Jace Ralls, Kemp Clendenin, Jane Sharp, David and Carol DeVries, Linda and Barnes Tatum, David Gibbs, James Bellamy, Will Willimon, Cathy Hurd, George Thompson, Cam West, Danny Morris, Skip Parvin, and Hank Keating. I have also been blessed by a number of editors who have encouraged me to write: Christopher Walters-Bugbee, Al Simonton, Kevin Rippin, and editors at Abingdon Press. In the last few years I have been privileged to serve with two other pastors, Susan Hubbard and Derry Barnhardt. I have been blessed personally by their pastoral gifts. This book could not have been written without their ministries to our congregation. Finally, I am grateful for the encouragement of my bishop, Charlene Kammerer.

This is probably a good time to acknowledge yet another debt to some of my teachers at Duke Divinity School, The University of Virginia, and Princeton Theological Seminary. While I won't list them by name, they know who they are. Chapter 3 in particular was developed as a portion of my Doctor of Ministry project at Princeton. I must also note the importance of two significant and extended continuing education experiences: the seminars of Kennon Callahan over a ten-year period, at Callaway Gardens in Pine Mountain, Georgia, and the workshops of Ed Friedman in Bethesda, Maryland. These latter two men have had a great influence on my life.

There have been other powerful experiences: Cursillo and Walk to Emmaus retreats and pilgrimages to Israel with groups of Christians and with interfaith and inter-racial groups of Jews and Christians. Much of what I know about the sabbath has come to me through friendships with observant Jewish friends.

There has also been a pilgrimage to Ireland with my wife; silent retreats at Dayspring in Germantown, Maryland; and journeys to Bolivia in South America and the Navajo nation in Arizona. I have experienced the richness of the Christian tradition in these and a number of other ways. This book is in part an attempt to repay that debt. These extended acknowledgments are my own attempt to be truthful about how ministry happens. It does not occur in a vacuum, and I am not a Lone Ranger. My ministry, for better and for worse, is woven together with these persons and places. They deserve much of the credit and none of the blame.

Finally, I am most in debt to my family. My wife, Pam, has been a Christian educator, a campus minister, a pastor, and an interior designer. Our older daughter, Liz, plays the viola and the baritone, and is a voracious reader of science fiction and fantasy novels. Our younger daugther, Abby, has gifts in singing and drama, and is one of the most compassionate people I know. There is a diversity of gifts even within our own small family, and I am grateful to share this life's journey with them. They are God's gifts of grace and joy to me.

Introduction

How This Book Developed and Why

When you send forth your spirit, they are created;
and you renew the face of the ground.
(Psalm 104:30)

Rekindle the gift of God that is within you
through the laying on of my hands; for God did
not give us the spirit of cowardice, but rather a
spirit of power and of love and of self-discipline.
(2 Timothy 1:6-7)

This is a book that has been in formation for a number of years. It comes out of the ordinary practice of ministry, in congregations ranging from very small to very large. Some of the theory underlying this book has come to me through reflection on what has gone wrong: a missed opportunity, a flawed way of seeing a situation, a tendency to be egocentric. In Christian tradition, this is called sin: sins of omission, *astygmatic* vision, the heart curved in on itself. Pastors are not immune to human sin. Sometimes we acknowledge our sin, sometimes we confess our sin, sometimes we learn from our sin.

This book has also come to me through additional reflection on what has gone right: a mission develops, a gift is shared, a group is formed, a journey is undertaken. In Christian tradition, this is called grace: we respond to the great commission, to go, preach, teach; we respond to the great commandment, to love; we respond to the call of the Lord, to follow. I offer this book to you in the hope that you will consider the importance of spiritual gifts in the pastoral ministry. There are many good reasons to work in the area of gifts. Some of these reasons are biblical. We think of passages such as 1 Corinthians 12–14, Romans 12, and Ephesians 4. We recover something of the experience of the early church when we move into the area of spiritual gifts. Some of these reasons may arise from our dissatisfaction with present forms of church organization. We have modeled the North American church in the image of a bureaucratic culture that has been in demise for at least a generation. Something is wrong—people do not want to spend time in meetings—and the language of gifts seems to offer a way out of our present structural impasse.

Our motivations to shape ministry around spiritual gifts may be well intentioned. If these motivations are grounded in love (1 Corinthians 13), we are on the right path. There are, of course, other reasons for working in the area of gifts, and some of these are not as helpful. We may enjoy tinkering with systems. Here restructuring community is not a way toward mission but a substitute for it. At times our investment in elaborate schemas related to gifts actually prevents us from the mission to which we are called.

We may also see gifts as a form of power. This is a language pastors speak better than others; it resonates with us. It is, to borrow a phrase, like having the "home field advantage." When pastors see gifts as an area in which they have a greater expertise than others, it can lead to abuse. When pastors do not share the ministry with the laity, the Body suffers. We may also have understandings of spiritual gifts that are more cultural than biblical, more individualistic than corporate. This book is an attempt to correct some of our working assumptions about gifts, in order that we might reclaim them for the mission of God. Again, the resources shared have come through reflections on mistakes and successes, on sin and grace.

How to Read This Book

I love to read. Sometimes on a summer vacation or on an airplane, I have longer periods of uninterrupted time to read. I may read the novels of Walker Percy, or the poetry of Mary Oliver, or the journals of Thomas Merton. Mostly, my time to read is in the midst of interruptions: a few minutes in the early morning when for some reason I wake up early; a few minutes in the middle morning in between writing a sermon and planning worship; a few minutes in the afternoon when someone has missed an appointment; a few minutes in the later afternoon when there is not enough time to accomplish a larger project; a few minutes late at night before I fall asleep, exhausted! I will assume that your reading times also come, in large measure, amidst interruptions. *The Gifted Pastor* can be read in the midst of the work; indeed, it is best understood alongside the data and experiences that can only be found there.

Chapter 1 contains a brief description of spiritual gifts in relation to pastoral ministry. Chapters 2 and 3 are discussions of the biblical foundations for spiritual gifts; each could serve as a resource for the church's teaching ministry about gifts. The fourth chapter contains the heart of my argument: that we cannot understand spiritual gifts apart from significant conversation partners. Said another way, we do not exercise spiritual gifts in a vacuum, and neither did the early Christians. Chapter 5 offers a very specific process to identify your own spiritual gifts. Chapter 6 offers some words of caution about spiritual gifts. Conciously or unconciously, many have done great harm to the mission of God through misuse, abuse, or neglect of spiritual gifts. Chapter 7 contains seven teaching sermons on spiritual gifts. Pastors who want to help their church's transition into this area will need to do the slow and gradual work of shaping perceptions of leaders and congregations through worship. I offer these sermons in humility, aware that every preacher speaks with his or her own voice, and out of a unique struggle with scripture and daily life. Chapter 8 is a glance at some (but not nearly all!) of the resources that are available to us in the area of spiritual gifts. I offer this material with some hesitation as well, for I contend that we do great harm to ourselves and our congregations when we adopt models or frameworks that have been "effective" or "successful" elsewhere. Reading through this section will simply give the reader a taste of the great variety of resources that are present among churches and those who lead them. Chapter 9 is a call for pastors to work on their own spiritual lives, as an act of what Ed Friedman terms "self-differentiation" and for the benefit of their own congregations. I look at the life and pilgrimage of Thomas Merton as a model for our own journeys toward gift discovery.

A final chapter is a sending forth, with seven suggestions for those who are on the journey in the discovery of their own spiritual gifts. These might be considered one at a time or by groups of clergy meeting together or as a focus for a day's work.

Finally, there is a blessing. My prayer is that reading these pages will awaken the reader to the gifts of God that are present in our lives.

For the task of teaching, chapters 2 and 3 will be most helpful.

For the task of preaching, chapter 7 will be most relevant.

For the ordering of congregational life and mission, chapters 6 and 8, in that order, will be instructive.

And for self-understanding, self-analysis, and spiritual growth, chapters 1, 5, and 10 will, I hope, supply spiritual food for the soul and the body.

Our pastoral fatigue is related to our need for renewal.

"Rekindle the gift of God that is within you," Paul wrote to Timothy. "Come, Holy Spirit," the psalmist prayed. When the pastor celebrates the Great Thanksgiving, she places her hands over the gifts of God, the bread and the cup, and she appeals to the Source of life and strength:

> Pour out your Holy Spirit on us gathered here,
>   and on these gifts of bread and wine.
> Make them be for us the body and blood of Christ,
> that we may be for the world the body of Christ,
>   redeemed by his blood.

Then she raises her hands into the air, and continues, to pray with even more boldness:

> By your spirit make us one with Christ,
>   one with each other,
>   and one in ministry to all the world,
> until Christ comes in final victory,
>   and we feast at his heavenly banquet.[1]

Because you are reading this book, I believe that you have some spiritual gift. As you read this book, remember that your ministry is also an outward and visible sign of the grace of God. Know that your preaching is an invitation to receive the grace of God. Be assured that your teaching is an introduction to a form of church life that is sometimes foreign to us. Recognize that your leadership will contribute to the unity of the church and the integrity of its mission.

There is much at stake! The Body of Christ accomplishes the mission of God in the strength of the Holy Spirit and through the form of the gifts of the Holy Spirit. Whenever the gifts of God's people are expressed, the Body of Christ becomes a sign of God's coming kingdom. Whenever the gifts of God's people are expressed, individuals experience grace. And whenever the gifts of God's people are expressed, we as pastors are reminded of why we were called into all of this in the first place!

Come Holy Spirit

Come, Holy Spirit . . .
I am never quite prepared to say
those words and really mean them;
for I might experience the full-force gale
of God's breath=wind=spirit
completely wrecking all that is orderly
in my life.

Come, Holy Spirit . . .
Perhaps I have fully worked out all my beliefs,
and then like a hurricane some crisis, some change,
visits me and knocks the foundations out from
underneath me, and I am shaken,
but I am alive.

Come, Holy Spirit . . .
When I am most comfortable in my religious life,
or when I am most confused in where I am spiritually,
God intervenes, and I know that there is . . .

A new *possibility*—dry bones can live,
a new *vision*—God's spirit will be poured out on all flesh,
a new *commandment*—God calls us to love one another,
a new *mission*—Jesus says, "As the Father has sent me,
so I send you."

Come, Holy Spirit . . .

—Kenneth H. Carter, Jr.

CHAPTER ONE

Spiritual Gifts and You

I will pour out my spirit on all flesh.
(Joel 2:28; Acts 2:17)

No one can say "Jesus is Lord" except by the
Holy Spirit. . . . To each is given the manifestation
of the Spirit for the common good.
(1 Corinthians 12:3, 7)

God has addressed us and continues to do so. To
know that God addresses "me" is to know that
God has spoken to me or to you, calling you by
your unique name. It is to know that our response
determines our destiny.
(Gordon Cosby)

Every Follower of Jesus Christ
Has a Spiritual Gift

This core truth is a corrective to many of our false
assumptions about gifts, about ministry, about life. Some
of us might believe that a few persons are truly gifted and
that the rest of us are not so endowed. If we believe that
we are in that number, among the gifted, we can become
elitist; and without knowing it, we convey an arrogance. If
we do not believe that we are gifted, we view ourselves as
deficient, void of talent or ability.

Some of us believe that only a few persons are ministers and the rest are recipients of services, or spectators.
If we count ourselves among the ministers, we overfunction, overextending ourselves; and we even grow resentful
or burn out. If we sense that we do not have a ministry,
we become passive (waiting to receive the ministry from

someone else) or critical (sensing that our role is to evaluate others in ministry).

Some of us live in ways that deny our true gifts, our natural abilities and passions. We reenact the parable of the talents in Matthew 25. We disparage any accomplishments in our past, we lower our expectations in the present, and we question future possibilities. At times, we are also unaware of the gifts of others. We find it difficult to trust persons around us to be competent or compassionate, and we are skeptical about their motivations and intentions.

This core truth—*that every follower of Jesus Christ has a spiritual gift*—is one that a pastor must reflect on, for it will shape his or her whole life and ministry. Gordon Cosby's discernment, that our destiny is bound to this question, is not an overstatement. *Do we believe that every follower of Jesus Christ has a spiritual gift? Do we believe that we as pastors have been given spiritual gifts?*

Our answers, of course, are lived out in the everyday practice of ministry. As we struggle with these questions we must acknowledge three important issues, ones that are foundational to this discussion and to day-to-day ministry. First, we may be called to give up control, or at least the *illusion* of being in control. Second, we progress in the spiritual life as we see people in their uniqueness. And third, we take steps toward the discovery of our own gifts, for we as pastors are also among the followers of Jesus!

Out of Control

If we are honest, as pastors, our hesitancy about the language and practice of spiritual gifts begins with the issue of control. When we begin to call forth gifts in others, we begin to lose control, or the illusion of being in control. Gifts are shaped by God's call, the needs of

God's mission, the sufferings of individuals and communities. Gifts do not fit neatly into our plans and schemes for ministry. Gifts flow from individuals who have been created in the image of God (Genesis 1:26).

Gifts are freely offered, by definition. They cannot be coerced or controlled, managed or manipulated. While this may seem a negative consequence of spiritual gifts, it actually helps us to lose our *illusion* of being in control.[1] The loss of this illusion reminds us of a liberating truth: that God is in control. Our functional atheism ("I am at the center of this ministry or mission") is counter to a conviction that God is in control. A belief that God is in control, in turn, shapes our practice of sabbath, grounds our understanding of stewardship, and speaks a word of judgment against our tendency to *overfunction*.[2] As Edwin Friedman, the family systems theorist often noted, our tendency to overfunction usually leads others to underfunction. Theologically, our trust in the God who is in control leads to the practical reality that others will share their gifts, if given the opportunity. Max DePree suggests that *"understanding and accepting diversity enables us to see that each person is needed. It also enables us to begin to think about being abandoned to the strengths of others, of admitting that we cannot know or do everything."*[3]

The pastoral ministry has taught me this truth in a couple of ways. For a number of years I have participated in Cursillo and Walk to Emmaus retreats. Aside from being wonderful experiences of grace, the weekends remind me again and again about the gifts of the laity. The retreats also teach me something about control: If a layperson can direct a Walk to Emmaus, he or she can also manage a church. And if the laity will manage or lead the church, pastors can serve as spiritual directors! If I am willing to give up some degree of control, or the *illusion* of control, I can practice in my own area of giftedness.

I have also developed a practice of sharing leadership in confirmation with lay leaders (in smaller churches) and with other staff (in larger churches) and have been drawn to the use of mentors with young people preparing for profession of faith and membership in the church.[4] I am amazed at the dedication of the laity in teaching, serving, counseling, and guiding processes that lead youth into a closer relationship with God. I find young people are drawn to the individual differences among a variety of leaders, and I often sense that the gifts of different persons complement each other.

Like most pastors, I am sometimes prone to *"do it myself."* My experiences in these areas are sometimes chaotic and surprising. But life is chaotic and surprising, and so is ministry. My desire to be in control is not helpful to me or to others; it limits the scope of the mission, and there is a personal and professional cost. When pastors overfunction, we are not willing to live *"out of control."* When we sense that everything does not depend on us, we live into the good news of the hymn, "leaning on the everlasting arms." God is in control.

Seeing People in Their Uniqueness

To see others in their uniqueness is a contemplative act. To see others in their uniqueness is to see their lives as *sacred texts,* texts as complex as biblical narratives we study and expound. To see others in their uniqueness is to search for another's potential for holiness. When we have lost the illusion of control, and allow God to be God, we begin to work with the deadly sin of *hubris.* Eugene Peterson writes helpfully that *"it is in this context of being most responsible, being obedient, that we most easily substitute our will for God's will, because it is so easy to suppose that they are identical."*[5] This hubris breeds an insensitivity to the uniqueness of others. Every pastor, to some degree, is infected with it.

To see others contemplatively is a difficult spiritual discipline for pastors. We develop, over time, a capacity to see people in more *functional* ways: she would be a great Sunday school teacher, he would be an excellent trustee (and yes, we do tend to stereotype people!). We begin with a role that needs to be filled, with a task that awaits completion. In this way we skim the surfaces of groups, understanding others only superficially as we search for a potential match.

When pastors are gathered in one place for an event, the discussion proceeds in this way. A larger group will be in a conversation, and there is talk about numbers in worship, goals met, accomplishments on the horizon. And we are mostly being truthful in these conversations. Then the groups break apart, naturally or perhaps by design. A different conversation emerges: We reflect on the difficulty of ministry; we confess our failures; we voice our uncertainties; we question our motivations.

The pastoral ministry is difficult. Indeed it may be that being a pastor is somewhat analogous to climbing a mountain: It is difficult and strenuous; there is often a temptation to give up; the destination ahead is not always apparent; and there are lots of folk at the base of the mountain offering advice. As the journey proceeds uphill, the companions become fewer; but there is an increasingly meaningful shared experience that is powerful and helpful. Peter Metcalf writes of the parallels of starting a business and climbing a mountain:

> You can't know what a climb is like without actually doing it. Everything else is just training . . . and if you decide there are no alternatives and you absolutely commit yourself to something, it is amazing how you can not only keep going way beyond what you thought you could do but also convince yourself and others that you can do anything.[6]

Consider two images for serving in ministry with

others: skimming the surface of a body of water or climbing a mountain. At times we have linked person and task, individual and role; but the relationship has been a shallow one: The gift is not a match with the mission, a passion is not present, a depth is missing.

The alternative is to see individuals in their uniqueness. To see persons as sacred texts is to know their histories as well as we know the texts that we teach and preach. In this way pastoral ministry becomes a contemplative act, as we see the potential for holiness within each person. In the Wesleyan tradition this has been described as the journey toward perfection, the renewal of the *imago dei* (image of God). The journey is one that demands all that we have. It is not unlike companionship with others on a strenuous uphill journey.

Individuals, of course, are diverse in nature and interest, in temperament and calling. I have caught myself leaving a parish, entering into a new one, and carrying along some plan or program that flourished in the last place, in which I am now an expert—or at least to a modest degree! More often than not, my scheme when transplanted into the new setting, no matter how clever or well intentioned, does not fit the new congregation. I have not taken the time to see individuals in their uniqueness, or to become acquainted with the culture in which these persons live.[7]

To take the time to be a contemplative pastor is to *listen*. Dietrich Bonhoeffer noted that:

> It is God's work that we do for our brother or sister when we listen to them. Christians, especially ministers, so often think that they must always contribute something when they are in the company of others, that this is the one service that we have to render. They forget that listening can be a greater service than speaking. Many people are looking for an ear that will listen. They do not find it among Christians, because

these Christians are talking when they should be listening. But the one who can no longer listen to his brother or sister will soon no longer be listening to God either. . . . This is the beginning of the death of the spiritual life, and in the end there is nothing left but spiritual chatter and clerical condescension arrayed in pious words. . . . Anyone who thinks that his time is too valuable to spend keeping quiet will eventually have no time for God and his brother or sister, but only for himself and for his own follies.[8]

To hear the stories of our people is to pastor in a contemplative way. If we have become deaf to the still, small voice (1 Kings 19) of God, Bonhoeffer would argue, it may be that the voices among which we serve have also become muted. In the Scriptures, the gifts of the spirit are always connected to call (see especially Ephesians 4). The call of God is to search for the uniqueness of the Spirit at work in the lives of God's people.

To contemplate the unique gifts of others requires that we step away, at times, from our own agendas. I once knew a woman who was a gifted therapist. Our congregation was in the formative stages of beginning a lay caregiving ministry that required mature leaders gifted in areas like listening, bereavement, and spiritual growth. I asked her to consider a leadership role, and she thoughtfully declined. *"I am a therapist all week,"* she responded; *"I love working with Girl Scouts. That is where God wants me to be."* My initial disappointment gave way, in time, to an appreciative acceptance. In the balance of her life she had found her way to serve through her daily vocation and in the church.

The Discovery of Our Own Gifts

As pastors, we live in the tension between the need for self-definition and the need to learn from others. It is absolutely essential that the pastor have a clear sense of where she or he is headed. In the theological tradition this is often defined as *authority;* in literature on church growth it is called *visioning* or *vision-casting;* in the language of family systems it is *self-differentiation.* The effective pastor has a growing range of authority. The effective pastor has an increasingly sharpened sense of vision. The effective pastor is able to define herself while remaining connected to the congregation. The effective pastor knows who she is!

There is a tendency to become enamored with models of leadership, church growth, and ministry that are hailed as successful or innovative. These models can be found in a number of settings, including the suburbs of Chicago, Los Angeles, and Dallas; and they are worth exploring. Both Willow Creek Community Church (Chicago) and Saddleback Valley Community Church (Los Angeles) have developed spiritual gift resources that are exceptionally well crafted.[9] *But these two churches should not be held up as examples of congregations to emulate.* They are highly unusual churches, planted in particular contexts, with remarkable leadership. Pastors who attempt to build Willow Creeks or Saddlebacks will, for the most part, bring frustration to themselves and a sense of failure to their people.

As pastors continue in the journey forward, we will discover a mission that is shaped by a variety of factors: the uniqueness of others and their gifts, the history and the culture of the congregation, and our own gifts. The effective pastor must learn from others, but clearly takes responsibility for his own identity.

Here the issue of spiritual gifts takes on crucial importance for the pastor. If the pastor is not aware of her own gifts for ministry, she will be tempted to strive for the gifts of others. *Much of the literature on ministry in our culture is written by individuals who have the gift of leadership.*

Their prescription for all that afflicts the church is more effective leadership. I want to suggest that there is an error in the diagnosis and in the prescription: *not every problem can be solved by more effective leadership,* and *not every pastor has the gift of leadership.*

Instead, there are a variety of gifts (1 Corinthians 12), and the presence or absence of those gifts create particular congregational cultures. It could be that a congregation suffers from a lack of shepherding, or from inadequate teaching, or from a failure to evangelize, or from an excessive emphasis on tongues. *"When the only tool we have is a hammer,"* Abraham Maslow is credited with the saying, *"we treat everything as if it were a nail!"* Our responses to others will always flow out of our gifts. The first step is to discover what those gifts are!

As you read this book, I invite you to reflect on the material in dialogue with your own ministry. How do you respond to the sermons? Do they seem liberating or confirming or guilt producing? Do the suggested practices seem familiar and possible or foreign and impossible? Are you drawn to the inventories as a way toward greater self-understanding? Does this seem to be an area that would help you to more faithfully serve others?

A couple of suggestions might help at this early stage. The Christian tradition, in its discussions of ordained ministry, has often spoken of an *inner call* and an *outer call.* You sensed an inner call to ordained ministry, and that decision filled you with grace and hope. But there was also an outer call. Lay members of the congregation of which you were a part sensed that same call; they perceived an emerging call in you, and other pastors did as well.

Perhaps you might return to the intersection of inner and outer call in the discovery of your own gifts. Do you sense a particular area of ministry or a set of tasks that seem to fit who you are and why you are drawn to this way of life? Is an inner call to give focused attention to the task of preaching met with a response that your preaching is helpful to individuals and faithful to the text? Is an inner call to visit with particular persons often connected to an outer call of gratitude?

Could our frustrations in ministry, indeed our propensity to burn out, be the result of our inability to hear the inner call to ministry? I once served four churches in a beautiful rural setting, where I followed a very popular and beloved pastor. He was in the latter stages of service; I was at the beginning. He left that assignment to enter into full-time evangelism. In my first two years I gave a great deal of energy to the work of evangelism. I tried to become an evangelist to those congregations, but I could not see much visible fruit. Instead, I was exhausted. I was trying to function, in sustained and ongoing ways, outside of my gift. I was not an evangelist. I was also not being honest with the people. And in attempting to offer a gift that I did not possess, I was not sharing what in fact I could give to them.

One afternoon I began to reflect on the pastors who had served those four churches. I went back over a period of thirty years, and many of the faces of the prior pastors came into focus. One was an excellent administrator. One was an activist. One had a compassion for missions. One was a shepherd. It occurred to me that if each of us would give our true gift to these people, they would indeed receive all that they needed, over time.

I had a love for teaching and study, having spent a number of years in divinity school and graduate school. The people had a desire to learn more about the Scriptures. And so I began to invest time in teaching multiple Bible studies, some short-term, others long-term, some in the mornings, and others in the evening, some surveys of the Bible itself, others closer examinations of particular books of the Bible. I found that people were growing spiritually. I sensed that I was enjoying myself. And, over time, I knew that I was giving the people in these churches my own unique gift. If there was some deficiency, and surely there was, God would compensate over time, as other faithful men and women were sent to serve that parish.[10]

The experience I have shared leads to a second suggestion. In your ministry you will find yourself in a variety of roles: administrator, pastor, celebrant, preacher, teacher, and evangelist are a few. There is no "typical" week, but think for a moment about a couple of recent ones. You no doubt spent time in each of these roles. As you reflect, which days and weeks leave you feeling tired and fatigued? And which time periods were energizing and gratifying?

When too much of our ministry is spent in areas outside our spiritual gifts, we descend gradually into fatigue. This is unfortunate, because pastoral ministry places enormous demands on the time, talents, and gifts of individuals. I have known friends serving rural churches who dream about the leisure of large congregations with staffs. I know large church pastors who yearn nostalgically for the days when ministry was simpler and less demanding. I am convinced that there are no greener pastures in which to minister. I am also sure that faithful ministry has been just as difficult in every era. What I hear among my good friends is an attempt to respond to a growing sense of fatigue.

When we discover our spiritual gifts and operate within them, our energy levels increase. The inner call to ministry connects with the outer call. We are reminded of the reason we entered into the pastoral ministry in the first place. We sense an organic relationship to others in the church who are also gifted. We read about congregations in the New Testament with both a realism and an excitement.

I have written this book to serve as a resource for pastors who know that something is wrong. We did not enter into ministry in order to be in control, or to *run* churches. We did not envision the immensity of human needs, the brokenness of communities, the dysfunction of congregations, or our own limitations. We have found ourselves in institutions that reward our overfunctioning. We have ignored the gifts that God has placed in others. We have buried our own talents. We have lost touch with the call to share our own gifts.

Being more effective will not help. Patterning ourselves after someone who seems to be successful is not the answer. These responses will only skim the surface of ministry. The New Testament teaches us a new language, a language of spiritual gifts. It is a language we learn with others, members of the Body of Christ. Remember: *Every follower of Jesus Christ has a spiritual gift*. To reach the mountain peak we will need every gift that is available. And as we journey up the mountain together, we will discover much about who we are, and where we are headed.

A Beatitude

Blessed are those who know they are traveling in the wrong direction.
God will lead them along a new path.

Blessed are those who know they are "works in progress."
God will shape them into something beautiful.

Blessed are those who know they are "unclean."
God will wash them in living waters.

Blessed are those who know their limitations.
God's law will shape their thoughts and actions.

Blessed are those who lack wisdom.
God will unite their beliefs with the gift of *faith*.

Blessed are those who give up trying to be God.
Christ will ignite their service with *love*.

Blessed are those who feel that God is distant.
The Spirit will infuse their lives with *hope*.

Amen.

—K. H. C.

CHAPTER TWO

Spiritual Gifts: The Classic Texts from Scripture

There are three classic texts in the New Testament that focus on spiritual gifts. They are 1 Corinthians 12; Romans 12; and Ephesians 4. I will reflect on them in that order, in a kind of pastoral commentary. If a pastor is to ground the life of the church in spiritual gifts, he or she will need to become acquainted with these texts and the issues that lie beneath them.

Spiritual Gifts and Community (1 Corinthians 12)

First Corinthians 12 serves as the beginning of a portion of Scripture that concludes at the end of chapter 14 and includes the chapter on love (13). When Paul notes that he does not want the reader to be "uninformed," he is stressing that the primary sign of the Holy Spirit is *love*, not glossolalia, or speaking in unknown tongues. Paul then reminds the reader that not all inspired speech is from God (12:2). As F. F. Bruce has noted, "Ecstasy or enthusiasm is not the criterion of spirituality; attention must be paid to the words spoken."[1] Those who persecuted Christians forced them to say Jesus was *anathema* (cursed), often as an entry into a sect. "Jesus is Lord" (12:3) is the most basic Christian creed. Note the important connection between Jesus Christ and the Holy Spirit. The Holy Spirit leads us to do those things that Jesus did.

In 12:4-6 there is a trinitarian structure: Spirit-Lord-God. The unity of the spirit is expressed in the diversity of gifts *(charismata)*, services *(diakonia)*, and activities *(energmata)*. Richard Hayes is helpful in noting that "Paul of course had no explicit doctrine of the Trinity; this doctrine was not articulated formally by theologians until hundreds of years later. The passage shows, however, that he *experienced* God as Trinity; he can describe the activity of God in the community in three synonymous parallel clauses as the working of the Spirit and of the Lord Jesus and of God."[2]

The gifts of God are given for the common good (12:7), and nine manifestations are listed in verses 8-10. The gifts are:

❑ Wisdom—*an insight born of maturity*
❑ Knowledge—*an inner apprehension of the truth*
❑ Faith—*trust and confidence in the miraculous work of God*
❑ Healing—*the work of God that brings about salvation and wholeness of body, mind, and spirit*
❑ Miracles—*the capacity to do mighty works*
❑ Prophecy—*the practice of building up the community*
❑ Discernment of spirits—*having a clarity about what is true and what is false*
❑ Various kinds of tongues—*a private prayer language*
❑ Interpretation of tongues—*the communal interpretation of someone's private prayer language*

Each gift has its origin in the one Spirit (12:11); thus there is unity within diversity.

Paul next begins a discussion of gifts through the image of the Body of Christ, in verses 12-26. This image had appeared earlier in the letter,

"Do you not know that your bodies are members of Christ?" (1 Corinthians 6:15)

"Because there is one bread, we who are many are one body." (1 Corinthians 10:17)
"All who eat and drink without discerning the body, eat and drink judgment against themselves." (1 Corinthians 11:29)

These scriptures refer to the interdependence of members within the Body of Christ, the church, and serve as a corrective to the privatization of our spiritualities and our temptation to withdraw from community. Because we have been baptized, the distinctions within the church disappear (1 Corinthians 12:13), and so we drink of the one Spirit, the invitation of Jesus to all who are thirsty (John 7:37-39).

Paul insists, in 1 Corinthians 12:14-22, that all parts of the body are important and necessary; in fact, the weaker parts of the body are indispensable! (12:22). Paul is appealing for unity, that there be no dissension in the Body. This requires an understanding of the interdependence of members of the church, in suffering and rejoicing (12:26). There follows a listing, in verse 28, of eight spiritual gifts, which do not correspond to the list of nine earlier:

❑ Apostles—*those who are sent by God*
❑ Prophets—*those who declare the mind of God in the present*
❑ Teachers—*those who instruct and guide others in the faith*
❑ Power—*see "mighty works" in list above*
❑ Healing—*see the first listing in 1 Corinthians 12*
❑ Helping—*extending compassion to the weak, poor, and vulnerable*
❑ Leadership—*those who order the life of the community*
❑ Tongues—*see the first listing in 1 Corinthians 12*

And in verses 29-30, there is a third listing of gifts, again slightly different. The chapter ends with an affirmation that the greatest spiritual gift is love. This chapter, so often read in celebrations of marriage, is better understood in its context. The spiritual gifts, taken to their extreme and expressed in their most dynamic form, are no match for the gift of love, which "builds up" (1 Corinthians 8:1).

Spiritual Gifts and Transformation (Romans 12)

It is helpful again to place this text in its context. In the first seven chapters of Romans, Paul reflects on the reality of human sin in light of God's grace, with full attention to our struggle to be faithful. Romans 8 marks a transition: There is no condemnation for those who are in Christ Jesus (8:1). The Holy Spirit sustains as we enter into our status as children of God (8:16), and we are encouraged in the promise that nothing can separate us from the love of God (8:28-38). Romans 9–11 is a meditation on a question close to the heart of the apostle: What will be Israel's destiny? Romans 12 marks yet another transition: How are we to live as God's chosen people, as God's adopted children, as those who are elected and included in the saving purpose of God?

In 12:1 Paul argues that life is shaped by the structure of God's grace. The sacrifice acceptable to God (our burnt offering) is the whole of our lives. This is our reasonable (logical) service, in light of all that has been given to us. We are then challenged: Do not be conformed to this world! Two recent translations are memorable:

> "Don't let the world around you squeeze you into its own mold." (J. B. Phillips, *The New Testament in Modern English*)

"Don't become so well-adjusted to your culture that you fit into it without even thinking." (Eugene Peterson, *Message*)

The transforming work of God in us helps us to discern the will of God, what is good and acceptable and perfect (Peterson translates this as, "God brings the best out of you, develops well formed maturity in you").

In Romans 12:3-13, Paul focuses on the experience of grace within the Christian community (compare with Philippians 2 and Ephesians 4). Remember: Christians have been adopted into a new "family" (Romans 8). This also rules out the spiritual pride that leads us to think that our gift is superior to the gift of another. In verse 4 Paul again argues for a diversity within the one body (12:4) that leads to our interdependence on one another (12:5). "We have gifts that differ according to the grace given to us," he insists in 12:6. Paul Achtemeier has noted that "The difference between Christians is not that some have spiritual gifts and some do not. The difference consists in the fact that not all have received the same gift."[3]

Another listing of the spiritual gifts is contained in Romans 12:6-8. Again, there is no hierarchy of gifts; each is important. There are seven:

❏ Prophecy—*see above*
❏ Ministry—*service to God's people in a practical way*
❏ Teaching—*see above*
❏ Exhortation—*encouraging others toward holiness*
❏ Generosity—*sharing out of one's own gifts*
❏ Leader—*see above*
❏ Compassion—*doing acts of mercy with cheerfulness*

After listing the gifts, Paul appeals to the importance of love. Eugene Peterson translates 12:9 in this way: "Love from the center of who you are" (*Message*). Christians are to love one another (12:10). A deepening understanding of spiritual gifts always has love as its foundation.

Here a word about love is important. Some of the literature on spiritual gifts, especially the works of Peter Wagner and Charles Bryant, draw too great a distinction between the *gifts* of the spirit and the *fruit* of the spirit. Love clearly is both a gift of the spirit (1 Corinthians 13) and a fruit of the spirit (Galatians 5). The priority of love in each case is obvious. Writing about the fruit of the spirit, Philip Kenneson notes:

> That love heads Paul's list of the Spirit's fruit is hardly accidental. Indeed, many Christian thinkers across the ages have insisted that the fruit of the Spirit listed by Paul are not nine separate fruit, of which love is simply the first. Rather, love—as embodied in Jesus Christ and poured into our hearts by the Holy Spirit (Romans 5:5), most fully reflects the character of God.[4]

Gifts are both expressions of who we are and what we do, our identities and our vocations. An appeal to "Love from the center of who you are" *(Message)* illustrates how the fruit of the Spirit shape the gifts of the Spirit.

Paul continues: "Don't burn out; keep yourselves fueled and aflame" (Romans 12:12 *Message*). In this context Paul is encouraging the Roman Christians to help the Jerusalem Church (12:13).[5]

Spiritual Gifts and the Equipping of the Laity (Ephesians 4)

In the letter to the Ephesians, we are introduced to the grace of God that saves us apart from our works (2:8-9). We are also confronted with God's ultimate plan and purpose, to "gather up all things in Christ, things in heaven and things on earth"(1:10). Chapter 3 begins with the word *therefore*; God's grace is the priority, our human response is the result. Theology precedes ethics. Spirituality precedes ministry. Here the letter's first three chapters are connected to the latter three with a word: *therefore*. In verse 1, we are challenged, in the language of the King James Version, to "walk worthy of the vocation wherewith ye are called."

The Message is just as vivid: "I want you to get out there and walk—better yet, run!—on the road God called you to travel." The calling is our vocation, our common task as the *laos*, the people of God. We live into our callings in humility, gentleness, patience. While not a translation, *The Living Bible* communicates truth: "Be patient with each other, making allowance for each other's faults because of your love" (4:2).

Patience is longsuffering (KJV) and persistent, and contributes to the unity of the Spirit within the community (4:3). The writer of Ephesians then lists the seven elements of this unity in 4:4-6: one body, one Spirit, one hope, one Lord, one faith, one baptism, one God and Father. Within this unity, however, is the insistence that we receive different gifts (4:7). They are:

❏ Apostle-*see above*
❏ Prophet-*see above*
❏ Evangelist—*one with a burden to announce the good news of Christ*
❏ Pastor—*shepherding God's people toward safety and growth*
❏ Teacher—*see above*

The purpose of these gifts is (1) to "equip the saints [Christians] for the "work of ministry" *(ergon diaconias)*, which could also be translated as "the task of servanthood" and (2) to build up the Body of Christ (4:11-12).

This text speaks directly to the authentic purpose of gifts of the spirit, and to the danger of their privatization.

Comparing the Texts

In reflecting on the texts related to spiritual gifts, it might be helpful to see them alongside one another. A simple description of each is included below.

1 Corinthians 12:8-40	*1 Corinthians 12:28-30.*	*Romans 12*	*Ephesians 4*
Wisdom			
Knowledge			
Faith			
Healing	Healing		
Miracles			
Prophecy	Prophets	Prophecy	Prophets
Discernment			
Tongues	Tongues		
Interpretation of Tongues			
	Apostles		Apostles
	Teachers	Teaching	Teachers
	Power		
	Helping	Compassion	
	Leadership	Leader	
		Ministry	
		Exhortation	
		Generosity	
			Evangelists
			Pastors

CHAPTER THREE

Scripture and Spiritual Gifts: Journaling and Self-Discovery

I, Paul, write this greeting with my own hand.
(1 Corinthians 16:21)

My assumption is that the story of any one of us
is in some measure the story of us all.
(Frederick Buechner, The Sacred Journey*)*

Spiritual Gifts: Seeing Ourselves in the Scriptures

Another way of reflecting on the relationship between the Scriptures and spiritual gifts can be found by asking individuals to discover themselves in the biblical texts. In a former congregation I asked a group of laity, over a period of four weeks, to reflect on specific passages of Scripture. Each day's journaling process included one passage from the Old Testament and one from the New Testament. The passages reflected the diversity of Scripture. I had chosen five spiritual gifts: teaching (Romans 12:7), prophecy (1 Corinthians 12:10), evangelism (Ephesians 4:11), service (Romans 12:7), and leadership (Romans 12:8), and matched them with prominent passages within the larger canon of Scripture. The responses are from daily journals kept by active members of one local congregation.

The Gift of Teaching
(Psalm 1 and Matthew 5–7)

Participants were asked to reflect on their understanding of Jesus as a *teacher*, and on their own experiences as teachers. One participant, who strongly identified with this model in her own life, described Jesus in the following way:

> Jesus is the master teacher. When reading the Matthew selection, His boldness, authority, obvious connection with the Hebrew Scripture, and His love are clear. He represents and translates the Law in a clearer way and does not soften or take away from it. The truth He represents and states gives the standard for my life, and the strength of His teaching says that this teacher means business and expects us to take the Christian walk seriously.

Another participant reflected on the teachings of Jesus within a wider context:

> Jesus as teacher: maybe a *mentor* in the broadest sense of the word. Jesus tried to teach his disciples "where they were." He challenged them to learn, to understand; but he knew where limitations lay and brought the disciples along as they were ready. Jesus lived what he taught—today we would say that he "modeled" what he wanted to see in the disciples.

Several of the participants commented only briefly on the role of Jesus as a teacher, if at all. Two described Jesus as a teacher against their own background as teachers, but did not seem to strongly identify that role as a calling in their own Christian lives. Several contended that one could live a meaningful Christian life without exposure to or participation in teaching experiences; another noted that "it's that struggling—and the prayers for understanding that I know from experience and wonder what rests in its place where there is no learning or study."

Sometimes individuals strongly identify themselves with these particular passages:

> I particularly found Matthew 5–7 to be exciting. . . . I like most of what was communicated in Matthew 5–7, but feel particularly close to Matthew 5:14-16. I used this passage as the theme for the Cursillo weekend when I was rector.

> Probably the Matthew 5-7 and Psalm 1. The Beatitudes have always been inspirational to me— they seem to make it simple and clear of what God expects and wants from us.

Another response speaks of the connection between the external call of the community, in affirmation of a gift and the internal call to teach:

> Yes! I have experienced both fulfillment and satisfaction as a teacher. I have experienced both in my profession and as a Sunday school teacher. It is hard to describe the good feeling of sharing new knowledge or understanding with others. To see the lightbulbs of understanding turn on in their faces is very rewarding and gives a feeling of a job well done.

The Gift of Prophecy
(Amos 5:21-24 and Luke 4:16-21)

At times in the Scriptures the requirements of God are in sharp contrast to the behavior of men and women. This was particularly present in the reading from Amos and in the prophetic statement from Jesus, also taken from the prophetic literature of the Hebrew Bible.

Participants were asked to reflect on the relevance of these passages in light of their own experiences.

One response seemed to catch the spirit of these readings and their "radical" character more than others:

> The hardest part of Christianity for Americans is Christ's teaching on riches, for we are all, even those of modest American means, fabulously wealthy by world standards or the standards of history. While Christ very clearly said "give away all you have and follow me," none of us does it. We try to live both ways, and go to church on Sundays in expensive suits. Africa and Asia are abysmally poor today, but the poverty and chaos there by the year 2050 will exceed anything we even imagine. How can we live with that?

Another wrote:

> The Christian is called to go beyond the "comfort zone" and minister to those who do not know Jesus, no matter who or where they are.

At times, prophetic passages are reframed in ways that fit our culture. Another participant proceeded to interpret these passages from a more therapeutic perspective:

> We are called not necessarily to the poor and oppressed, but to the poor in spirit and ones who are captive to the world and oppressed by depression, illness, and self-indulgence.

Another participant, reflecting on the same passages, interpreted them in quite different fashion:

> A true Christian is set apart—does not fit with society—and yet cannot remove herself from living in

community. I guess that means I have to get over wanting to be like everybody else—not be different in some radical, "unaccepted" way. I don't think my journey so far has allowed me to explore the implications of life as a resident alien. I haven't ventured down that road where decisions might be difficult and sometimes painful. Could it be that life lived "against the grain" is the way to a life which is empowered, free, and moving in the journey?

The set of passages most resonant for me are the ones referring to the Christian faith as going "against the grain" of society and the passages about Jesus' servanthood. . . . The fully realized Christian life requires us to go beyond . . . passive activities to take a more active part in leading and sharing.

Several of the participants seemed to acknowledge the importance and essential nature of this model of the Christian life, and wrote movingly about seeing these texts in the lives of friends or acquaintances who were serving as missionaries, in urban ministries, and in political roles. None, however, strongly identified with this model; this could be due to a tendency toward humility or to the church's orientation toward the priestly rather than the prophetic.

The Gift of Evangelism
(Genesis 12:1-3 and Matthew 28:16-20)

These scriptural passages place God's command to be a blessing and the commissioning of the disciples within the context of a life of outreach and evangelism. Participants were asked to reflect on their own feelings about the word *evangelism* and about ways that these passages are being fulfilled by God's people today. One participant perceived the crux of the issue:

> Can a person be a faithful Christian while holding little interest in passages like these? I think 95 percent of Christians consider *themselves* faithful without evangelizing. I think most people don't really come to terms with their Christianity and live their faith—allowing it to significantly change their behavior.

Another responded:

> Evangelism. . . . I think of telling others about Jesus and this is exciting to me. That word scares some, turns some off; but to me, its what the church is all about or should be. Christians are responsible to the call of Christ to tell others about him. God has called faithful ones from the beginning of time to be a "light to the nations." It is not an option, and faithful Christians take this call seriously. All the families of the earth can be blessed with abundant life, joy, salvation, as each Christian responds to this command.

Other participants expressed differing readings of these texts:

> I struggle with passages like these because I think I never want to impose my views on others, especially if they are made to feel uncomfortable. I don't want to "turn people off" to Christ—so my verbal witnessing is not so great. I guess I choose, rather, to live a life that is somewhat focused on God—but the Bible says "Go out and teach them." I can't ignore passages like this, but I am not too comfortable talking about my relationship with God and Jesus. Maybe I'm not mature enough in my faith.

The following entry expresses discomfort with these texts, for different reasons:

I have negative feelings about evangelism if it means go out and try to convert everyone to Christianity. I think its arrogant of us to think we have the one true way of inner peace and happiness; and it is demeaning to others whom we are judging as wrong because their beliefs are not our beliefs. . . . I really am uncomfortable with the concept of the chosen people, or that some are better than others or that "God likes me best." I think one doesn't have to embrace these passages to be a faithful Christian, but ironically living a life of faith is potent evangelism!

The following response indicates a perception that this day's reading is normative for that person's Christian experience:

The scriptures . . . from Genesis and Matthew are the most exciting. First of all, the two references show God's eternal intention—that all who know him should tell others. This intention was shown in the beginning with Abraham and has been the same through the ages. Second, each reference shows God's personal involvement in the call and response—Go and I will be with you.

Most of the remainder of the entries ranged somewhat in the midst between these two extremes—between those who embraced evangelism and these texts as central to the Christian life and those who, for a variety of reasons, did not sense them to be important in their own experiences.

The first two responses listed above seem to indicate that the participants see this model as one that is essential to the Christian experience. Interestingly, participants were asked to think about other individuals whose lives, in their estimation, embodied this biblical model. Another participant reflected on the life of another:

> I think _____ fits my model of a true evangelist. He seeks truth, but doesn't let questions deter him from living out his faith—in actions, in conversations, in witness. He represents the "thorn in the side" that doesn't allow people like me to become complacent.

Identification with these texts was made difficult by the stereotype of "evangelism" and those who are "evangelists" in our culture. The following illustrates a common response:

> "Evangelism" has a decidedly negative connotation because of the frailty and misguided focus of many prominent TV evangelists.

For this reason identifications with these models are probably underrepresented in mainline churches; those who identify with this model have moved beyond these stereotypes; and if the identification has taken the form of a call, the response is usually carried out without a great deal of affirmation.

The Gift of Serving
(Isaiah 41:8-10, 42:6-9, and John 13)

The guiding paragraph on this day posed two biblical passages for the participants, that focused on the role of servanthood among God's people. Individuals were asked to reflect on the meaning of servanthood for themselves and for others. One participant discerned this model to be a particularly compelling one:

It is with an issue like this that I see one distinguishing characteristic that sets Christians apart from the world: We serve because Christ was a servant and clearly told us to do this in memory of him. We are not to serve because it makes us feel good or serves as some kind of therapy. We are not to serve because it is a good example for our children. We are not to serve because it will make the wheels of society turn more smoothly. We serve because Christ was a servant.

Another participant struggled with these same issues, if communicated in a somewhat different fashion:

Sometimes I enjoy doing something so much that I begin to think my motivation must be purely selfish. . . . It is important to me that, while carrying out these activities [ministries], the focus of attention stays on God and not on me. I am very uncomfortable with receiving personal credit for doing God's work. As a result, I make a good "Indian" and a lousy "chief." I am very comfortable with the role of servant if I can carry out the role fairly invisibly. I tend to lose interest in the task if too much attention turns my way. I believe servanthood is important to the church because the church has a responsibility to inform the membership of their roles as servants. The church further should provide many opportunities for the members to be servants.

This response also places a great emphasis on the importance of servanthood, but reflects on this model in a more personal way. There is also a sense here that there are varying ways of being in service (1 Corinthians 12:4); several of the participants, for example, interpreted their service through particular acts of ministry:

My calling appears to be that of Isaiah 41:6—to see that justice is done on earth.

I have felt called to be a servant of God in many
ways. . . . I enjoy teaching adult Sunday school class
. . . being a Stephen minister . . . the lay witness
program.

How am I called to be a servant of God? I believe I
am called to teach. I believe I am called to teach our
congregation about evangelism.

In these responses the participants interpret their models of the Christian life through the *lens* of servanthood.
Individuals are often reticent to identify with the servant
model—this is likely due to the virtue of humility that is
characteristic of servanthood—but the struggle with the
model, in an in-depth way as seen above, indicates that
this model is a compelling vision of the Christian life for
the person. The following *self-identification* clearly articu-
lates this vision:

By now this should be fairly obvious . . . when I
read these passages I say "Whew!" There is a place
for me in the scheme of things! Its very exciting!!
I've had so many wonderful opportunities to serve
it's really hard to pin down one experience. I did
have an opportunity to serve a family member who
was in trouble. This was very meaningful to me. . . .
I'm quite comfortable with these scriptures.

The Gift of Leadership
(Exodus 18 and 2 Timothy 2:1-2)

The final day of reflection on particular passages of
scripture and models of the Christian life focused on the
subject of leadership. Individuals were asked to consider
the qualities of leadership in themselves and others in
light of these texts. One participant responded in the following way:

The Exodus and Timothy passages remind me that the good news is *not* concentrated in one person's hands but rather open to all and many must be leaders. The effective church leaders are, to me, the people who are committed—who develop relationships with people and who risk themselves by stepping into areas and issuing a call for action or contemplation or renewal.

Another participant emphasized the inner life in relationship to leadership:

> I think an important quality is to be prayerful about your leadership and direction. It's important to have a sense of being led by God. Wisdom is necessary.

It is significant that these participants wrote explicitly about leadership and its internal, spiritual, and theological dimensions: call, personal risk, prayer, wisdom, relationships. Another person drew the distinction between leadership understood in this way and leadership *roles* in the church:

> In some areas, I am a leader in the church, but I don't see myself as a "mover and shaker" in the sense of committees, chairperson of committees, or dealing with the big decision-making process. Leadership for me has come in the realm of teaching, prayer, and caregiving.

Others drew from insights in the two scripture passages to evaluate their own leadership capacities and those of others:

> An effective leader in the church [possesses] the people skills to identify and nurture talent; and the willingness to "let go" is also an important leadership skill.

Another person did not see these qualities in reflecting on her own Christian life, but acknowledged them to be facets of leadership in the church:

> I do not feel that I am a leader. No, not particularly. As stated above I'm much more comfortable in the role of "Indian" rather than "chief." I generally lack the assertiveness to be a good leader, and I'm not particularly strong in motivating others. However, I do think I am fairly strong in carrying out work assigned to me.

This response may be an accurate self-evaluation of a person's understanding of his or her leadership abilities; it fails to take into account the compelling relationship between servanthood and leadership. The participant clearly sensed a linkage by drawing from a previous entry from that day's journal, but did not make the connection between the two models of the Christian life.

Another participant wrote:

> The passages about . . . leading relate best to my Christian experience. I guess being chairperson of an important committee (was) an experience that tested me and affected my spiritual journey. I didn't enjoy it, it challenged my skills and faith (why me? why not me?), it forced me to act at risk in persevering despite obstacles, but I think the impact was positive.

The process of asking individuals to keep a journal related to key passages of scripture, and then discover themselves in them may be more helpful than the inventories that list varying spiritual gifts and definitions of them. I found the journal entries to be rich descriptions by men and women of their Christian experiences. I also felt that the participants were able to connect their own spiritual gifts with a variety of ministries.[1]

As pastors employ the concept of spiritual gifts in local congregations, they will benefit from a basic knowledge of the classic texts related to gifts, and from listening to individuals who engage with these texts and discover themselves in them! This is the ministry of forming disciples.

We Are Disciples

We are disciples.
We are learning, growing, stretching.
The learning can be arduous, the growth difficult,
the stretching painful.

But we are disciples.
We are called to be disciples.
In the midst of working, earning a living,
raising families, there was a call:
to move beyond ourselves,
to love God with heart and mind and spirit,
to leave behind nets and follow.

A Rabbi once talked about mustard seeds
and prodigal sons and lilies of the field
and laborers in a vineyard.
He called disciples who were drawn
to the power of his stories.
We love those stories,
what they meant, what they mean.
We are drawn to the logic, to the surprise,
to the mystery, to the Word in the words.

That Word orders our lives, guides us, disciplines us.
At times we are able to be disciplined,
to respond from deep within.
At other times we are not.
As disciples we are always in the process of being formed,
like clay in the potter's hands.

As disciples we are always in the process of being reformed,
like a church that belongs to God.

As disciples we are learning:
what it's all about, where it's all leading,
what it all means.
Answers to these questions are not given to the curious;
they are opened, revealed,
to those with ears to hear and eyes to see,
to a generation that does not seek a sign,
to those who hunger and thirst for God.
As disciples, we realize that we have much to learn.

—K. H. C.

CHAPTER FOUR

Spiritual Gifts: Some Conversation Partners

I thank my God every time I remember you, constantly praying with joy in every one of my prayers for all of you, because of your sharing in the gospel from the first day until now.

(Philippians 1:3)

The Christian seeks neither autonomy nor independence, but rather to be faithful to the way that manifests the conviction that we belong to another. Thus Christians learn to describe their lives as a gift rather than as an achievement.
(Stanley Hauerwas, A Community of Character)

Spiritual Gifts and Servanthood

Have this mind among yourselves, which is yours in Christ Jesus, who . . . emptied himself, taking the form of a servant.

(Philippians 2:5, 7 RSV)

Christ has no body now on earth but yours,
   no hands but yours,
   no feet but yours.
Yours are the eyes through which the compassion
   of Christ
   is to look out on a hurting world.
Yours are the feet with which he is to go about
   doing good.
Yours are the hands with which he is to bless now.
            (A Prayer of Saint Teresa of Avila)

From the hand of a Christian pastor, writing years later to his first congregation, a congregation that he had helped to found, we have the letter to the church at Philippi. There is, even in this first-century congregation, a two-cell fight, between Euodia and Syntyche. We understand two-cell fights in congregations: newcomers and old-timers, boomers and builders, those who give the money and those who spend the money, those who want to look at stained glass and those who want to look at words on screens.

This letter is filled with practical advice: Paul knows the congregation—and himself—well; and he warns them against the deadly sins for any community: self-centeredness; conceit, grumbling. One thinks she is the center of the universe; another is puffed up with pride; another is what we would call a "whiner." Paul pleads with these folks to strive toward the fruits of the Christian life. And at the end of chapter 1, Paul encourages the Philippians to let their lives be "worthy of the gospel of Christ"; in addition, he appeals to them to stand "firm in one spirit, striving side by side with one mind for the faith of the gospel" (Philippians 1:27).

Into this appeal for unity Paul inserts a hymn, which begins with the words "Have this mind in you which was in Christ Jesus." Unity was critical for the early Christian movement, just as it is important for us. "Make my joy complete," Paul pleads, by coming together, by working toward unity. And unity is possible because of an even greater reality present among us: *servanthood.* Come together, Paul says; have the mind in you that was in Christ Jesus, who *emptied himself.* Paul is talking about humility, about being there for others, about, to use the profound phrase of Henri Nouwen, the "downward mobility" of God: Although Jesus was equal with God, he did not choose to cling to that, to claim that, but instead emptied himself.[1]

So much of our lives is wrapped up in status or pecking order. I remember one of my first classes in divinity school. It was an ethics seminar. Most of the students were doctoral students. I was not. There were just a few of us there. The professor began by going around the room, asking about our previous schools. The first guy spoke: "Harvard." "Ah," the professor responded. The second person, a woman: "Colgate." "Oh," the professor spoke, "I know Dr. So and So." This went on. It came to me. I told him where I had gone to college. He looked at me as if to say, "I've never heard of it." I felt like the least kosher person there.

Pecking Orders

A few years later, after I had served briefly in an appointment and then had gone to graduate school, I was appointed to four churches in a rural county. Some of the most faithful Christians I have known were in those churches. I remember the annual gathering of pastors in my denomination that year. "Welcome back," they would begin. "Where are you going?" I would answer. Some would then look at me with a long silence: "Four churches—what did you do wrong? Who did you offend?"

Pecking order. And I can tell you that I was not the first chicken. Pecking orders die hard. I can go to a preacher's meeting; there are pecking orders there: How big is your church? How fast is it growing? What is your budget? How many people are on your staff?

Pecking order. That is the way of the world. But the good news is that it is not the way of the Lord. Jesus is equal with God—that's pretty high up on the pecking order; and yet he empties himself and becomes a servant. He chooses to be one of us. He chooses to be our servant. He chooses to wash our feet. That is who Jesus is.

And that is also who we are when we choose to be the people of Jesus. We choose to be servants. We choose to follow Jesus on the way to the cross; we choose to carry the cross. When we choose to be a Christian, we choose to be a servant. I read an article in our local newspaper about the merger of the two hospitals. One of the themes in the piece was the impact on the workforce. What would this mean to the staffs? A housekeeping person was interviewed. *"I'm not worried,"* she said; *"there's always going to be a mess to clean up. Somebody's going to have to do it."*

There is, in every culture, a struggle to get to the top of the pecking order; but there is always a need for a servant. And so, maybe the questions for the church should be, "How many servants are in our church? How many people are we serving? What is the next area of service to which we should invest ourselves?"

Servant Leadership

Robert Greenleaf, in his book *Servant Leadership,* talks about the difference between people who want first to lead and then at some point make a conscious choice to serve, and those who are servants first and at a later time find themselves being called forth to lead. Jesus was a servant leader. He was a servant Lord. It is necessary to remember the ordering. He emptied himself and became a servant. And because of the depth of his servanthood, God has made him our Lord. And when we affirm his lordship, we are also called to live as servants. Jesus the servant comes to be our Lord. Jesus the Lord calls us to serve. Lordship and servanthood: they are woven together. So much so that Jesus said "the greatest among you must be your servant."

Have this mind in you which was in Christ Jesus, who emptied himself, who took the form of a servant. One of the most profound books of recent years is by a management consultant named Peter Block, entitled simply *Stewardship: Choosing Service over Self-Interest*. He writes:

> Ultimately the choice we make is between service and self-interest. . . . The antidote to self-interest is to commit and to find cause. To commit to something outside of ourselves. To be part of creating something we care about so we can endure the sacrifice, risk, and adventure that commitment entails. This is the deeper meaning of service. . . . Our task is to create organizations we believe in and to do it as an offering, not a demand. No one will do it for us. Others have brought us this far. The next step is ours. Our choice for service and community becomes the only practical answer to our concern about self-interest.[2]

The call to service is the call to follow Jesus. The only church that will survive into the next millennium will be the church that takes the form of a servant. The calling forth of spiritual gifts is closely aligned to the words of the housekeeper: *"There's always going to be a mess to clean up. Somebody's going to have to do it."* As we share our spiritual gifts, we take the form of a servant, we make Christ visible, we reverse the pecking orders, and we lift high the cross.

Unity was a concern for Paul in writing about spiritual gifts (1 Corinthians 12–14). Unity was also a concern for Paul in writing about servanthood (Philippians 2). The way to unity is through servanthood. The way to spiritual power is through servanthood. The way of servanthood is the way of Jesus. It is the way that leads to life.

God calls forth our gifts. We wonder about pecking orders. We are in good company. James and John wanted to sit at the right hand of Jesus, in his glory (Mark 10:35-45). Whoever would be greatest, the Lord insisted, must become a servant.

Servanthood, Spiritual Gifts, and a Therapeutic Culture

The church is recovering the emphasis in Scripture on spiritual gifts. But it is essential that spiritual gifts are always linked to service. The exercise of spiritual gifts may indeed result in self-fulfillment; but that is, at best, a by-product. It is important to note the power of the therapeutic culture in which we live and serve. In a penetrating essay entitled "The Psychological Captivity of the Church," Greg Jones argues that "psychological language and practices have become more powerful than the language and practices of the gospel, not only in the culture but also in the church. As a result, we have translated and reduced the gospel into psychological categories. Such reduction has altered and distorted the practices of the church."[3] The exercise of spiritual gifts has at times been defined as a form of self-fulfillment; in fact, it may be a form of self-denial. This tension is expressed in the Covenant Renewal Service, patterned after the Wesleyan tradition, which is found in both *The United Methodist Book of Worship* and in the Disciple Bible Study. The invitation has a power and directness:

> Commit yourself to Christ as his servants.
> Give yourselves to him, that you may belong to him.
> Christ has many services to be done.
> Some are more easy and honorable,
>   others are more difficult and disgraceful.
> Some are suitable to our inclinations and interests,
>   others are contrary to both.
> In some we may please Christ and please ourselves.
> But then there are other works where we cannot please
>   Christ except by denying ourselves.
> It is necessary, therefore,
>   that we consider what it means to be a servant of
>   Christ.

Christ has many services to be done. There are a variety of gifts. Pastors will have the experience of working, for a time, in a setting that is outside their gifts. A need emerges: The pastor serves in a congregation whose pressing need is administration; the preacher serves in a congregation that cries out for shepherding. In these settings, we serve the larger mission after the example of Christ.

We are called to serve. Life is lived at its best when we are serving. That is who we are. Have this mind in you which was also in Christ Jesus. God wants nothing more, and the world looks for nothing less. Richard Foster invites us to pray this simple prayer, "Lord Jesus, bring me someone this week whom I can serve." And then he comments: "This is a prayer that God loves to answer."[4] I would simply add that God answers this prayer through the offering of our gifts!

Our difficulty in serving is often connected to our need to be in control.

When Helping You Is Helping Me

When I go to help someone,
I discover that I am the one
who is being helped.
When I allow myself to be a servant,
I learn again that I am being served.
Sometimes I think I am the host,
but in reality I am the guest.

In God's kingdom, there is a great reversal
of expectation. As I reach out to others,
I become aware that God is reaching out to me.

I like to be in control.
I am comfortable in being merciful.
But God calls me to be compassionate,
to share in the sufferings of others,
as Jesus, in his suffering, shared with me.

God invites me to be a servant,
even in the midst of suffering.

And Jesus teaches me that, in helping others,
I am the one who is being helped.
—K. H. C.

This movement, toward servanthood, is expressed powerfully in the hymn text by Brian Wren:

Great God, in Christ You call our name
And then receive us as Your own,
Not through some merit, right, or claim,
But by Your gracious love alone.
We strain to glimpse Your mercy seat
And find You kneeling at our feet.[5]

Spiritual Gifts and Small Groups

They devoted themselves to the apostles' teaching and fellowship, to the breaking of bread and the prayers.

(Acts 2:42)

The local congregation is the future of the church. The renewal of the church finally depends upon what happens at the grass-roots level. And renewal at this level awaits, it seems to me, the conscious reclaiming of the gifts of the Spirit on the part of the laity. These gifts, which in the New Testament are always identified as signs of the coming kingdom of God, are given to the whole people of God for ministry, for diakonia.
(Jurgen Moltmann, Hope for the Church*)*

There is in our time a redefinition of the church around the concept of small groups. This has sometimes been called the metachurch model, borrowing from the work of Carl George, and it is also influenced by the ministry of the Church of the Saviour, led by Gordon and Mary Cosby and chronicled by Elizabeth O'Connor, in the model of the mission groups.

Much of the literature about small groups focuses on the model as a means of caregiving, in contrast to the solo pastor as the sole caregiver. There is truth in this insight, and the development of the Christ Care (small group) model by the Stephen Ministry is a testament to the growing appreciation of this movement.

I want to focus on another dimension of small groups, and that is their potential for calling forth spiritual gifts. The gifts of God are given to and for the sake of the community. This is noted in the book of Acts: And a sense of "awe came upon everyone, because many wonders and signs were being done. . . . and day by day the Lord added to their number those who were being saved" (Acts 2:43-47).

A helpful voice in the literature on small groups has been that of Gordon Cosby, cofounder of the Church of the Saviour. Each mission group in the Church of the Saviour was birthed by response to a call. For example, one of the mission groups was the Dayspring Mission group. For a number of years I traveled with groups to the Dayspring Retreat Center in Maryland, just west of Washington, D.C. Dayspring has served as a context for the spiritual renewal of thousands of pilgrims over the past thirty years. At the heart of Dayspring is a core group of gifted individuals. One, Carol, has the gift of hospitality. She makes all who enter into that environment feel welcomed and loved. Others have the gifts of prayer, teaching, service, prophecy, and shepherding. The inward journey of the mission group has helped those called to Dayspring to discover their spiritual gifts. The outward journey has led these same individuals to share their gifts.

Gifts are identified in other ways through small groups. A notable example is the Disciple Bible Study. Because men and women have shared the life of an extended small group, they come to see the gifts in their brothers and sisters in Christ. In an atmosphere of support and accountability, they also become more confident in their own gifts and potential for ministry.[6]

The Life Cycle of Groups and Spiritual Gifts

It is one thing to talk about small groups and what they help to bring forth; it is another to work toward or experience the creation of a group. Those with experience in development of small groups know that group process can be difficult. I want to offer a brief description of how small groups form.

First, there is *inclusion*. At the most basic stage in life's pilgrimage, individuals are asking the question, "Will I be accepted in this group?" Before a pastor begins to express his or her gifts in a congregation, this question must be resolved. Before newcomers, even those with significant leadership experience, begin to offer ministry to a congregation, they will want to know if they are going to be included.

The second stage is *shared experience*. Human beings have been created for community, just as God in the Trinity is communal. We long for shared experience. We come to know each others' stories. We laugh and weep together. A wise pastor expressed it to me this way: "The ministry only begins when you have gone through the seasons a few times with your people!" There is no substitute for shared experience.

Where there has been inclusion and shared experience, a third stage is *trust*. We begin to trust each other. We are willing to take risks, to be vulnerable. In my fourth year in one congregation, I began to call together individuals who might serve persons with HIV/AIDS. The timetable is not as important as noting that, in our setting, I felt that people needed to come to know me, and trust me, before they entered into a ministry that was new for us, and one that carried with it dimensions of personal and private history. We are hesitant to offer our gifts when we do not feel included, when we do not know one another. We offer our gifts in confidence and hope when we trust those who serve with us.

A fourth stage is *task*. The task is the expression of our gifts for the common good. Many of us are task oriented. We sense that we know what needs to be done. Needs cry out for ministry. The lost have not heard the good news. The isolated long for shepherding. The hungry yearn for the teaching of the word of God. These are tasks. But we do not begin with task. We begin, in the theory of group process, three steps back.

When a person is included and there has been a shared experience and trust is developing, the task can be accomplished. This framework is crucial for the exercise of spiritual gifts. Any ministry that focuses on spiritual gifts must take into account the reality of how groups form.

A Parable

My experience of small-group theory has been consistent across a variety of assignments. In serving as pastor of four small rural churches (with worship attendance ranging from fifty to one hundred), each congregation functioned as a small group. Often the groups were shaped by family heritage, close proximity to one another, and a time span of decades. The smaller groups within these church groups, whether they were choirs, circles, or Sunday school classes, had moved through all four stages. They functioned very efficiently; indeed, this was their strength. The only weakness was in allowing new persons to enter into the groups. They were so bonded that change did not come easily!

I once served as a mentor to a group of student pastors who were serving rural churches of approximately the same size. At one point a pastor expressed frustration about his parish's resistance to change. I shared with them a simple parable.

A church, over a period of about ten years, had been served by capable and faithful seminary students. For two years they had been led by a pastor with a strong sense of the moral and ethical dimensions of the gospel. The next pastor served three years; her ministry was shaped by experiences in the charismatic movement. In the next two years this small rural church welcomed as pastor a man who had been a business manager prior to the call to ordained minister, and he felt his task there was to organize the church structurally and administratively (even though it was a small parish!). In the prior three years, the pastor had been difficult to classify. There had been no discernible shape to the ministry.

As my friend Ken Callahan would say, the church had successfully resisted each of these directions in ministry. Their response was due to a couple of factors. First, in each case there had not been enough time to move to the stage of either *trust* or *task*. The members of the congregation were unwilling to progress beyond their shared experience with the pastor, and this was most likely due to their recent history. Second, in each case the pastor seemed to have little interest in the culture of the congregation or the gifts that God had placed in it. The pastors were projecting their own gifts onto the people they had been sent to serve. For this reason, the resistance was in fact not a sign of faithlessness; it was actually a necessary response to ensure the future of the congregation's mission.

Group process—inclusion, shared experience, trust, task—takes time. As we move through group process, we are allowing for the growth and development of spiritual gifts, our own and those of others. It is essential to remember that our gifts cannot flourish apart from those of others, even those that seem to be less important

(1 Corinthians 12:22). Without small groups, spiritual gifts become individualistic. This would seem an unlikely outcome, given the corporate definition of gifts in the letters of Paul; but it happens. We refer to *"my gifts for ministry,"* as if we were speaking of "my story/soap opera," or my personal preference.

Spiritual Gifts and Community

Spiritual gifts are always given to the community, and they are best expressed within small groups. In literature on management, the growing emphasis is on teams. In literature on leadership, there is a movement away from the "great man" or "great woman" theory. We might find ourselves in awe of the giftedness of a public figure, but the mission of God is always accomplished through a variety of gifts.

I have served remarkably different congregations over a period of about nineteen years: a four-point charge; a large regional church as one of three pastors; a new congregation; again, a large regional church as senior pastor. A common thread running through each has been the vitality of small-group life.

In one rural church a group of dedicated laity had felt marginalized by the denomination and sensed a need for renewal. Ten men and women embarked on a thirty-day spiritual discipline that included rising at five-thirty in the morning, reading Scripture, journaling, praying, meeting weekly, and engaging in one unselfish act for another person each day.

In one large congregation, a group of couples have met for years on Monday evenings. They have supported each other through the raising of children, through shifting economic climates, through spiritual mountaintops and valleys, and now, after three decades, through the deaths of lifelong friends.

In another congregation, a group of women emerged who focused on creativity and the spiritual life. In the process they supported one another, and deep and lasting friendships resulted.

In each small group there was a process of inclusion, shared experience, trust, and task. Each task was slightly different—in one case it was spiritual renewal; in another it was support; in another it was personal and spiritual fulfillment. In each case spiritual gifts were exercised: hospitality and wisdom, exhortation and healing. God uses small groups as instruments of grace in our lives. God also uses small groups to develop the spiritual gifts that we share with one another.

The house church movement in the book of Acts was the setting for spiritual gifts. The early Christians had all things in common. They shared a rich common life, in the apostles' teaching and the fellowship, in the breaking of bread and the prayers (Acts 2). God's intention from the beginning was for a spiritual body of believers, not for individual and disembodied spiritual seekers.

There is one additional truth: Those who come to know us in small groups can best identify our gifts. Over the past ten years I have shared in the leadership of a number of Disciple Bible Study groups. I often sense a hesitancy among individuals to name the gifts of others or to hear their own gifts called forth. But as the Disciple Bible Study process concludes with a process for the identification of gifts, I am amazed by the profound depth of gift identification and recognition. I am convinced that it comes only through shared participation in a small group over a period of time: There has been inclusion and shared experience; now there is trust and task. Through Disciple, those who have come to know us in small groups can become patrons of our gifts, to borrow the language of Gordon Cosby. They can affirm us and call us to share our gifts in confidence and with hope.

Love One Another, As I Have Loved You

A Christian is a person who loves God and loves the
neighbor.
A Christian is a person who strives to receive God's greatest
gift, love.
A Christian is a person who follows Jesus, the love of God
incarnate,
made flesh, made visible, among us.

I believe in love. I know about love.
I can talk about love, sing about love,
think about love, search for love.

And yet there are times when I have difficulty with love.
I like to be the one who defines what love means.
I like to be the one to place limits on love.
I like to be the one to set the conditions for love.

Followers of Jesus are immediately gifted with love.
Followers of Jesus are immediately confronted with love.
"Love one another," Jesus says, "as I have loved you."
Jesus feeds me when I am hungry; that is love.
Jesus clothes me when I am naked; that is love.
Jesus touches me when I am unclean; that is love.
Jesus welcomes me when I am a stranger; that is love.
Jesus heals me when I am ill; that is love.
Jesus forgives me when I sin; that is love.
Jesus restores me when I am broken; that is love.

I would like to love others as Jesus loves me,
but what if . . .
They reject the food and clothing that I give,
or do not deserve them. . . .

They draw away from my touch, or refuse my hospitality . . .

They cannot break free of illness,
will not accept my forgiveness,
do not desire reconciliation?

Then I have been offered a gift,
but that gift has been squandered,
buried, rejected.
And in some sense I feel rejected also,
because my love comes from deep within me.
My love expresses who I am.

As I live in Christ, I feel rooted, secure, connected.
As I live in Christ, my weaknesses, failures, shortcomings
become, through faith,
my strengths, victories, achievements.

As I live in Christ,
I find that I am drawn to his people, the body of Christ.
As I live in Christ,
I bring Christ to others.
As I live in Christ,
I see Christ in others.

In my love for others
I come to understand something of Christ's love for me,
for . . .

I reject the bread of Christ;
I want to clothe myself;
I fear the touch of the master's hand;
I would like to make my own place;
I dread the process of healing;
I question the possibility of reconciliation.

I know how I have responded to the love of Christ;
how will others respond to my love?

As I offer the gift, I take a risk.
As I offer the gift, I am vulnerable.
As I offer the gift, I become a new person.
This is precisely why love is so frightening
and so wonderful.

The reality of love points me toward connection, life, growth.

As I love others,
I am connected to them;
I experience communion with them.

As I love others,
I know life as it is intended to be lived.
As I love others,
I grow as a person.
I am called out of my own preoccupations and concerns
to consider the hurts, needs, and longings of others.

When Jesus calls me to love,
he invites me into an experience
that is both joyful and threatening.

As I respond to this call, to love others,
I discover that I am required to give,
perhaps more than is humanly expected;
but I sense as well that I will receive
far more than I expect or deserve.

—K. H. C.

Spiritual Gifts and Stewardship

*When the LORD your God has brought you into
the land that he swore to your ancestors, to
Abraham, to Isaac, and to Jacob, to give you—a
land with fine, large cities that you did not build,
houses filled with all sorts of goods that you did
not fill, hewn cisterns that you did not hew, vine-
yards and olive groves that you did not plant—
and when you have eaten your fill, take care that
you do not forget the LORD, who brought you out
of the land of Egypt, out of the house of slavery.*
(Deuteronomy 6:10-12)

Upon leaving the first session of a seminar in graduate
school, I asked the student who had sat beside me about

his college studies. "I majored in both religion and economics," he replied, "so I guess I'm qualified to begin my own cult." The intended humor in his response was an indication of the uneasy relation between spiritual faith and material possessions, God and mammon. The conversation was echoed years later as I was in the midst of a conversation with a friend at annual conference. "The stewardship campaign," he said, "is a necessary evil. I like to do it early in the fall so that we can be done with it." The implication, again, is that ministry and money, discipleship and stewardship, are worlds apart.[7]

Christians have always struggled with our relationship with the material world; note many of the discussions between Paul and the church at Corinth and the primary themes of John's Gospel. Practically, Christian leaders for centuries organized their strategies of participation in the world around the evangelical counsels: poverty, chastity, and obedience. These issues—money and possessions, sexuality, power and authority—continue to shape our life together as God's people. And they have everything to do with how we express our spiritual gifts.

Light and Darkness

Despite their similar titles, Richard Foster's *Money, Sex and Power* and Philip Turner's *Sex, Money and Power* are marked by significant differences in their methods and conclusions about the role of money and possessions in the Christian life. Richard Foster, one of the most helpful guides of the Christian spiritual life in our time, calls for a "creative" examination of the relationship between money and Christian faith as an alternative to monastic renunciation and Puritan industry. He locates two divergent streams of teaching in the Bible. Texts such as Matthew 6:24, "No one can serve two masters. . . . You cannot serve God and wealth," emphasize the dark side and portray money as a potentially dangerous power, while passages such as Matthew 25:14-30 (the parable of the talents) stress its light side and regard material blessings as a gift from a gracious God.

The distinction between light and darkness will resonate with the experience of most pastors. We have probably known persons whose possession of money or knowledge about it has resulted in actions that have been destructive to the fellowship and mission of the church. We have also, if we are honest, questioned our own motives for ministry, reflected on the wisdom of knowing about the financial giving patterns of church leaders, and questioned our own attitudes toward money. There is a dark side to money.

And yet money can be a vehicle of blessing; indeed, dare I say it, it can be an outward and visible sign of an inward and spiritual grace! God can use the generosity of individuals and congregations in ways that allow the Kingdom to be experienced: there is healing of the sick, feeding of the hungry, good news to the poor (Matthew 11). Every pastor has observed the light side of money in the life of the congregation.

Money can be both a blessing and a curse, and it can produce both greed and selflessness. Foster offers Christians counsel in "conquering" the dark side of money, as well as encouragement in the practice of generosity and graciousness. His interest is in guiding individuals toward faithful strategies with regard to money—listening to biblical teachings about money, siding with people against money and things, denying favored treatment of the privileged, and offering support for and solidarity with the poor.

Individuals and Congregations

Foster's distinction between the light and the dark sides of money is helpful, but ultimately it fails to reflect the complexity of the matter. There is light and darkness in each of us and within our congregations. The moral theologian begins his analysis there, with a reflection on the moral life of the Christian community in its economic practice.

Primarily concerned about the ordering of monetary relations within the church, Philip Turner, on the other hand, grounds his social ethic upon the provocative assumption that it is the nature of God to "give, receive, and return." He says that because "presence, reciprocity, giving, receiving, and returning define the deep structure of both divine and human life," then all discussions of economic relations derive from an immanent understanding of the Trinity, which serves as the "foundation of anthropology and of all social ethics."[8] For this reason, theology is not something we do once the stewardship campaign is completed; theology is "fleshed out" as we engage in the practice of Christian stewardship.

The target of Turner's discussion is the church. He is convinced that by ignoring the significance of economic relations within the household of faith, the church has erred in two significant ways. First, we have failed to see the potentially powerful influence that the church's own economic witness might have on society. Second, our evangelistic mission to the world is inevitably hampered by the absence of just and gracious economic relations within the church itself; the truth of the gospel is, after all, to be displayed not only in speech but also by actions. On this point, Ken Callahan's observation that there are often caste systems within local churches is particularly relevant.

A Steward's Prayer

O God of creation,
you have made us in your image;
you have placed gifts within us;

you have sustained us with bread and wine;
you are always with us.

O God of compassion,
you have delivered us from bondage;
you have spoken to us through prophets;
you have offered your life on a cross;
you are always with us.

O God of judgment,
you have met us in the hungry;
you have cried to us in the homeless;
you have touched us in the untouchable;
you are always with us.

O God of hope,
you have placed before us a promise;
you have shown us a new heaven and a new earth;
you have made clear a vision;
you are always with us.

As your stewards, O God,
help us to use our gifts wisely and joyfully;
move us to the healing of relationships;
prod us toward courageous speech and action;
and remind us that your kingdom,
which we now glimpse only in part,
is yet to be.

Help us as stewards to be a part of its coming,
through Jesus Christ, our Lord.
—K. H. C.

Spiritual Gifts and Sabbath

*Remember the sabbath day, and keep it holy. Six
days you shall labor and do all your work. But the
seventh day is a sabbath to the LORD your God;
you shall not do any work. . . . For in six days the*

75

> LORD *made heaven and earth, the sea, and all that*
> *is in them, but rested on the seventh day; therefore*
> *the* LORD *blessed the sabbath day and consecrated*
> *it.*
>
> (Exodus 20:8-11)

> *One of the ways God has provided for us to stay*
> *aware of and responsive to him as the determining*
> *and centering reality of our lives in a world that*
> *doesn't care about it is by sabbath-keeping. At*
> *regular intervals we all need to quit our work and*
> *contemplate his, quit talking to each other and lis-*
> *ten to him. God knows we need this and has given*
> *us a means in sabbath—a day for praying and*
> *playing, simply enjoying what he is.*
>
> (Eugene Peterson, Working the Angles)

Creation is a mystery before which we stand in awe and reverence. The creation passages, in Genesis 1 and 2, portray the miraculous beginnings of life. Two separate accounts of creation are recorded, and in the second one God creates the heavens and the earth and then causes a mist or flood (Genesis 2:6) to fall upon the earth. Then God forms man from the dust of the ground and breathes into his nostrils the breath of life, and man becomes a living soul. The breath or spirit of God is breathed into men and women, and there is life.

I came across an interesting discovery in preparing a sermon on the meaning of *sabbath*. In the fourth commandment, which speaks of God's rest (Exodus 20:11), the word used literally means "to catch one's breath"—which is what God did after creating all that is for six days; then God made the seventh day a holy day.

The Sabbath as Refreshment and Renewal

A sabbath day, a sabbath experience, is one in which we catch our breath. It is a time when activities cease, even the activities of which the apostle Paul speaks in 1 Corinthians 12:5. Some of us may have negative opinions about the sabbath from our early years. I remember Sunday, our sabbath day, as a day on which we could do very little. We couldn't play ball, mow grass, shop, or see movies. It was a day to stay home and do as little as possible. I remember, for the most part, the don'ts, the negatives, the legalisms.

In recent years, however, I have come to see the sabbath in a more positive light, as a time for refreshment and renewal. Old Testament scholars note that the original sabbath was a day not of worship but of rest. A well-known pastor recounted a conversation with a layman active in his church at the end of a particularly long Sunday of church activity: "I'm sure glad there is only one day of rest per week," the layman observed. "I'd burn out if we had to go through two days of rest like this every seven days."[9]

I don't know when you experience the sabbath each week. Sunday may not be the day that rest is possible.[10] For the Christian pastor, it cannot be a day of rest. The fact remains that we must find times of rest in the midst of activity and work. "The busiest and most active organ in the human body is the heart, which beats seventy to seventy-five times a minute, thirty-six million times a year; and yet those beats always happen on an exertion-rest rhythm. There is exertion, and there is rest. This is the delicate balance of the human heart, and of life."[11]

Recall Paul's discussion of the body in relation to spiritual gifts (1 Corinthians 12). Consider the health and well-being of your own body. Sometimes gifts are shared, expressed, active. Sometimes gifts rest, for a time or a season. But there is more here than a principle for living. The Scriptures teach us that this is the way that God acts, the way God created all that is. God's work was followed by a time of refreshment and renewal.

The Sabbath as Witness

The charge to rest, to refuel, is a sermon that many of us need, whether we hear it from our spouses, our physicians, or a preacher. But there are more reasons to keep the sabbath. Keeping the sabbath is also an act of faith, a gesture of trust. The sabbath is an important part of our heritage as God's people.

In *Finally Comes the Poet*, Walter Brueggemann has noted two crucial motivations for keeping sabbath in an age of restlessness: We are called to rest as God rested in the act of creation (Exodus 20:11), and we are to remember, in the midst of the sabbath, "that liberation permitted new life" (Deuteronomy 5:15). Brueggemann observes that "the two motivations, creation in Exodus 20 and liberation in Deuteronomy 5, hold together the ordered life of God and the just intent of human life. To keep Sabbath is to engage in an activity that holds together, sacramentally, the life of God at rest and the life of the world in liberation."[12]

To observe the sabbath is to affirm our faith in a God who created the world and holds it together, even as we rest. As we sing in the children's hymn, "He's got the whole world in his hands."

I have a rather brash friend who supervised a seminary intern. The student arrived at the beginning of the summer, met the people, and became involved in the work. Toward the end of July my friend informed the student that he was planning to take a week of vacation. A day or two before his departure, the student came forward and expressed some anxiety about my friend's leaving and her ability to care for the church in his absence. Finally, he said to the student, "This church has been here for 150 years, and you won't be able to kill it in a week!"

"He's got the whole world in his hands," we sing as children. "The earth is the LORD's and all that is in it," the psalmist cries out (Psalm 24:1). As we observe sabbath, we express our belief that we belong to this God and to no other. As we observe the sabbath, we acknowledge that God is the giver and the sustainer of life, and that its continuing survival and prosperity does not depend on us. As we observe the sabbath, we remember that God created the earth in six days and rested on the seventh

Someone recently remarked that God's people have never had to work seven days a week. This person concluded that if we labored six days, God would provide for the seventh just as God did with the children of Israel on their journey. Here Brueggemann's connecting of restlessness and greed is particularly perceptive. Sometimes we must miss a sabbath; even Jesus said that the sabbath was made for us and not the other way around. But if we find that we are making no room for rest, for the presence of God in our lives, then we may be too busy. And our busyness may mask a lack of trust in the God who provides.

The Sabbath as a Reminder of Our Limitations

The sabbath is a reminder of our human limitations. We cannot do it all. We never could, and we were never expected to do everything. A focus on spiritual gifts, without sabbath, can quickly degenerate into a form of workaholism. In addition, we must occasionally rest so that others will use their gifts. In the language of family systems, if we persist in overfunctioning, others will learn to underfunction.

Sabbath is also relevant to a discussion of spiritual gifts in the context of mission. We cannot wait until all the work is done before we accept the gift of sabbath. The great theologian Karl Barth put it this way:

> If man has created neither heaven and earth nor himself; if he does not owe his existence to himself, but to the will and act of Him who bestowed it on him without his slightest co-operation; if his ability to work is

not his attainment and therefore his own property, but a free gift; if his obligation to work is not his invention but God's commission, then he cannot and should not imagine that what is going to become of him, his future and that of his fellow-men, lies in his own power.[13]

God has placed limits on us, even as God places limits on our bodies. To everything there is a season, a time, and a purpose under heaven. There is a time for work, and as Christians we are called to be faithful, diligent, hardworking, and dependable so that no one can speak ill of our faith. But there is also a time for rest, and as leaders in the community of faith we express this faith in observance of the sabbath. God created on the first six days. This is God's gift to us. On the seventh day God rested, blessed that day, and made it holy. This, surely, is God's gift to us as well.

Catching My Breath

The devil has a device called "busyness,"
by which he deceives Christians into thinking they are doing the
will of God.
Meister Eckhart, Thirteenth Century

I catch myself speeding, pacing,
my body ahead of my spirit, the whirl
of sound and light around me, getting there
too quickly for some unexplained reason . . .

On the seventh day God rested.

And then I am pulled over, written up,
and there is guilt and shame, more to do,
and there is punishment, and brokenness
of body or spirit . . .

Remember the sabbath day, and keep it holy.

I find myself cruising, but out of control,
neglecting the temple that is my body,
ignoring the pattern of my breathing,
abandoning the holy places, deaf to the Word.

If you seek me with all your heart, you will find me.

When I live in Christ, I discover a balance: I work and rest,
inhale and exhale, laugh and mourn, pray and act.
I forgive and I am forgiven. I serve and am served.
I love and am loved.

The rhythm of Jesus is simple:
He calls us to receive the grace of God.
And he calls us to share the grace of God.
It's simple . . . as simple as breathing.

Let everything that breathes praise the Lord!
—K. H. C.

Spiritual Gifts and Mentors

*Peace be with you. As the Father has sent me, so I
send you.*
(John 20:21)

*Keep on doing the things you have learned and
received and heard and seen in me, and the God of
peace will be with you.*
(Philippians 4:9)

*I received from the Lord what I also handed on to
you.*
(1 Corinthians 11:23)

I have always been drawn to the Gospel of Matthew. It
is a "teacher's" gospel, and I have always been drawn to
the gift of teaching. Jesus says, "Go . . . and make disciples of all nations, baptizing them in the name of the

81

Father and of the Son and of the Holy Spirit, and teaching them to obey everything that I have commanded you. And remember, I am with you always, to the end of the age" (Matthew 28:19-20).

The impact of this passage of scripture has been enormous. It is often called the Great Commission, although those words are a relatively recent editorial comment about the passage.[14] It has ignited men and women toward lives in service of the gospel. Scholars have argued that it is the key to understanding the whole of Matthew's Gospel. Jesus, in Matthew, is a teacher, a discipler, a mentor. In Matthew 5–7, the Sermon on the Mount, he interprets the law. He is the new Moses, his authority comes from God.

As you listen to these words, you can see the pebble being dropped into the water. You can see the ripples going out, across time and into the future. Jesus, at the end of his earthly ministry, standing on a small mountain in Galilee, is teaching, discipling, mentoring.

It may take some imagination to read this text in light of the role of mentoring, but consider: Jesus is calling his disciples to acts of service within the Body of Christ. This text is the link between his own earthly ministry and the ministries described in the letter to Paul. In the same way, the mentor is a link between his or her own ministry, much of which may have been in the past, and that which will take place in the future.

Mentors encourage the expression of our spiritual gifts. One of my mentors was a man named James. My wife, Pam, and I served with him in a summer internship. He affirmed us when we did something right, and gently led us forward when we messed up. He was a teacher, a discipler, a mentor. He was a source of inspiration. A lifelong bachelor, he served under a bishop who did not value the gifts of single pastors. And so James remained in this parish for ten years, an act of neglect by the hierarchy but an unintended blessing for the congregation and community. James was known as the community pastor. He had the gift of being a good shepherd, and through his actions and words he taught me to become comfortable in entering into the lives of individuals and families as a pastor. He stood with me when I was ordained, and I still feel the ripples in the waters of the stones that he dropped in his ministry.

A mentor shapes the future of another. This is very much a part of the language of our rituals of baptism, confirmation, and membership. It is also important for those who serve as pastors to take the act of mentoring seriously.

Mentors are involved in the very important task of "calling forth gifts," to use the language of Gordon Cosby. This call begins, he suggests, with the gift of the person as he or she is.[15] In other words, it is not for their function within an enterprise or cause, but for their personhood. This is a radical perspective, but the reader will recall how amazing it is to be known and accepted and loved apart from performance. This we recognize as the grace of God. Mentors in some way are instruments of the grace of God in our lives.

Early in the ministry I served as an associate pastor with James. James had been in ministry in large congregations for a number of years. He had developed strong ministries in several churches, and he was respected and loved. He had lived long enough to resolve many of his own "ego needs" (he would have used that language); and he could focus on people, not as a means to some end but in their own struggles and joys. At his memorial service years later, his lifelong friend gave the eulogy and noted that James had been a patient nurturer of associate pastors. That was true, in my experience, because he saw gifts in me that I did not see and accepted me not only for what I could contribute but also for who I was, imperfections and all.

The power of mentoring in this way, of course, is that when we receive grace, we want to respond with the sharing of our own gifts. An environment is created; an internal motivation is cultivated. Managers produce compliance. Mentors call forth gifts. There is a difference.

Mentors also keep us connected to the grand questions of purpose and meaning. They bring gifts of wisdom to us. Edward Sellner describes the mentor as a "soul friend," and quotes Saint Brigit out of the Celtic Christian tradition: "Anyone without a soul friend is like a body without a head."[16] Busy pastors will know what it is like to go through seasons of life without a soul friend. There is isolation and loneliness. Sometimes the sheer demands of ministry lead us to the sense that we are going through the motions, without the time to reflect on where we are going or why.

Another important mentor to me has been David. For years David and I met occasionally for breakfast. He is a management consultant, highly regarded across our country. One day we were having a conversation about life and work. I had read something that said, in effect, that we now live in a culture of permanent white water. White-water conditions, for those who have been canoeing or kayaking, are times of rapid change and strong turbulence. And our culture seems to be like permanent white water: Everything is rapidly changing. Nothing stays the same. Everything is unpredictable and becoming more complex—permanent white water.

He thought for a second, and then commented. "Maybe so," he said, "but no one can exist for a long period of time in permanent white water. We have to have times to rest and float and to see beauty." David was offering me the gift of wisdom: a mature perspective on the journey of my own life and ministry.

Mentors are men and women—sometimes clergy, sometimes laity—who enter into our lives at strategic times along the way. Sometimes they affirm. Sometimes they correct. Sometimes they ask the right questions. Sometimes they see what we do not see. Mentors, at their best, know our gifts and encourage us to employ them. In reading the Gospels, it has occurred to me that only Jesus could have seen the gifts that were possible in each of the disciples. His mentoring of an unlikely group of characters was critical to the birth of the Christian movement in the world.

I Am with You Always

If I could recapture a feeling I once had,
If I could make it through the maze,
If I could remember the destination that lies ahead:
Would I see you in a cloud by day
or a fire by night?

Jesus says, "I am with you always."

I know that you lead me and guide me, O Lord,
that you sustain me and renew me . . .
And yet my hardness of heart
is difficult to penetrate.
I have erected a barrier, a wall,
that you will not climb or destroy.

Jesus says, "I am the good shepherd."

My spiritual strategy is no puzzle to you:
I keep you at a distance—
close enough to see the reflection of your light,
far enough away to manage on my own,
without you.

Jesus says, "I am the light of the world."

Do I believe in you?
Have I forgotten that you love me?

Place your hand in mine, and I will walk with you.
Plant your word in my mind,
and your light will be upon my path.
Deepen your spirit within my heart,
and I will know, once again,
the joy of your salvation.

—K. H. C.

CHAPTER FIVE

A Process for Spiritual Gift Identification

I appeal to you, brothers and sisters, by the mercies of God, to present your bodies as a living sacrifice, holy and acceptable to God, which is your spiritual worship. Do not be conformed to this world, but be transformed by the renewing of your minds, so that you may discern what is the will of God—what is good and acceptable and perfect.

(Romans 12:1-2)

When you claim your strengths, you claim God's gifts. Whatever strengths and competencies you have, you have because God has been and is now, this very moment, stirring in your life. God's compassion and spirit are extraordinarily present in your life. Your strengths are gifts from God. God invites us to claim our strengths.

(Kennon Callahan, Twelve Keys for Living*)*

What is my spiritual gift? You may be asking yourself that question. Or perhaps you have a hunch, a clue, a sense of where your gifts lie. Perhaps this has come by trial and error. Rick Warren of the Saddleback Valley Community Church argues that we can only know our gifts as we use them in mission. Perhaps others have identified your gifts through words of affirmation and gratitude.

What follows is a process for the identification of spiritual gifts. It is a discernment process shaped by the work of Danny Morris, formerly of the Upper Room in Nashville, and Chuck Olsen, who leads Worshipful-Work in Kansas City.[1] Together they have blessed the church with wise and helpful reflection on the process of corporate discernment. Their work, I suggest, can also help us to identify our spiritual gifts within the Body of Christ, the church.

As you move through this process, you will at times need the guidance of the Christian community. Perhaps a trusted colleague or a friend or a coworker from within the laity, or a member of your Pastor-Parish Relations or Oversight committee will join you in the exploration of your gift or gifts. At other times you will need to do the work alone. The process will not be one that can be completed in an hour or a day or a few days. You will need time to enter silence, to explore options, to rest with decisions. Take your time. Be patient.

There are ten steps. You might use a journal or a legal-size notebook to record your responses. No one else can really do the work of spiritual gift identification for you. Your own grasp of where you are gifted, why, and for what purpose is of utmost importance.

Framing—Moving Toward the Specific

In framing the discussion of spiritual gifts, we move from the topic in general to asking the question, "Is this my spiritual gift, yes or no?" A word about how critically important this is: While it might seem like a luxury to spend time in reflecting on whether or not we have a particular spiritual gift, the opposite is actually the case. It is crucial that we identify our gifts as pastors. So much of our time is spent in particular ministries: preaching, teaching, visiting, administering, praying, evangelizing. Sometimes we enter into a relationship with a church that is actually crying out for a particular gift: For example, a large church is in need of healing after a scandal involving its last senior pastor; how important it might be for an interim pastor, or the successor, to have the gift of healing, to recognize the importance of healing, and to express that gift among people in need of it.

We have to begin somewhere. Choose a spiritual gift, one that seems to be within the sphere of your interest, passion, or competence. You will know this from prior experience and from feedback you have received from others. Choose one spiritual gift, and begin by framing the question:

God, is my spiritual gift in the area of _____, yes or no?

You are seeking to discover your priority in life. And as you enter into this exercise you do so in the spirit of the Lord's Prayer: *Thy kingdom come, thy will be done.* You are seeking to know God's will for your life. You are attempting to discover the mind of Christ. And you are becoming attuned to the Spirit's yearning for the church and her mission.

Grounding—Naming Our Assumptions

In grounding we continue to explore our gifts by naming our assumptions and stating our guiding principles. It is helpful to speak aloud or to write down matters that are essential to us, or to a congregation, but that may go unspoken. For example, the process of spiritual gift identification is more grounded as we focus on issues like:

The greatest need of our community right now is _____.

If the pastor were to do one thing well, it would have to be _____.

People come closer to God's will for their lives as they

_____.

You will discover the importance of grounding as you consider your own assumptions about the faith. For example, those with the gift of preaching assume that individuals are transformed by hearing the message. Those with the gift of teaching give priority to our understanding of the faith and to the explanatory power of the Scriptures. Those with the gift of hospitality are convinced that individuals must be welcomed into community as an integral aspect of the encounter with God. Those with the gift of evangelism focus on God's gift of unmerited grace and the necessity of our human response. Those with the gift of administration see chaos and disorder as harmful to the ongoing work of the kingdom. Each spiritual gift can be connected to an assumption that we have about human nature and the purpose of the church.

As you identify a spiritual gift, attempt to spell out the assumptions that are implied in your concept of it. Grounding will also help you to remain specific, to articulate the boundaries of your gift's expression. What is the purpose of this gift, and what is outside its purpose? Authentic grounding about spiritual gifts includes corporate prayer and can best be pursued in an environment of safety, support, and sometimes even confidentiality.

Shedding—Confessing Our Sin

In shedding we come to grips with the reality of our sin, our distorted vision and our will to power. Shedding is "naming and laying aside anything that will deter the person or group from focusing on God's will" in relation to the spiritual group under discussion.[2] It is the process of relinquishment, letting go, or indifference, which is not apathy but consent to God's will and purpose.

This is difficult work, for the individual and for the community, and it helps to say a brief word about the nature of God. We believe that God is One who creates us in his image (Genesis 1:26), and calls us to share ourselves and our gifts with others. Since God has created us, God will know best what our gifts might be and how they might be employed.

Our difficulty arises when we become egocentric—we assume that we ourselves know what is best for us, for our churches, for our ministries. And at just this point we can "get in the way" of God's creative work in us. Shedding drives us back to a dependence on God and a reliance on God's will. The question is,

If I have discovered a particular gift of God in my own life, would I be willing to develop and share that gift, even if doing so seems unnatural or difficult?

Olsen and Morris ask the right questions: "Are we willing to let something die to give God room to start something new? What will we lay aside or leave behind so that we will be open to new gifts of grace or new expressions of ministry?"[3]

Rooting—Discovering Ourselves in Scripture

In rooting we seek to unearth biblical passages that relate to our spiritual gifts. For many this comes easily: We felt a call to ministry because someone connected a passage of scripture with a compelling invitation to serve in some way, perhaps as an evangelist or as a teacher or as a preacher or as a counselor. The process of identifying our spiritual gifts deepens as we focus on a biblical image, verse or theme.

- Those who serve think of Jesus washing the feet of the disciples (John 13).

- Those who teach recall the Sermon on the Mount (Matthew 5–7).

- Those who administer remember Moses and the advice given him by Jethro (Exodus 18).

- Those who pastor will recall the image of the Good Shepherd (John 10).

Reflect on a spiritual gift that seems to be coming into focus for you. Can you think of a biblical image, a text, a theme from Scripture that provides a foundation for that gift? For me, an important image is of Jesus' teaching in John 15:5:

"I am the vine, you are the branches. Those who abide in me and I in them bear much fruit, because apart from me you can do nothing."

This verse and those that surround it have been significant to me in framing my ministry: It is important that we are connected to God; it is also important that we are connected to one another. I have tried to keep this biblical image at the center of my mind and spirit, especially in pastoral relationships, in preaching, and in teaching.

Listening—Hearing the Voice of God

In listening we enter into the practice of Psalm 46:10:

"Be still, and know that I am God!"

Listening as a tool for spiritual gift identification will take place in some setting of silence. As we become better listeners to God, in the silence, we also become more attuned to what others are saying to us. Remember the statement of Dietrich Bonhoeffer:

> Many people are looking for a listening ear, [but] they do not find it among Christians, because these Christians are talking when they should be listening. He who can no longer listen to his brother will soon no longer be listening to God either. . . . This is the beginning of the death of the spiritual life. . . . Anyone who thinks that his time is too valuable to spend keeping quiet will eventually have no time for God or his brother, but only for himself and his own follies.[4]

Many individuals encounter the call of God and experience the discovery of their gifts in silence. In the busyness of our usual routines and activities, we are sometimes successful in crowding out the voice of God. If we can listen deeply and attentively, we will hear a word about God and about ourselves.

Practically, listening might occur in one of these ways:

- A period of early morning quiet, for about thirty minutes each day for a week

- A period of one day, apart from usual activities, perhaps at a retreat center or a park, by the ocean, or in the sanctuary of a church, with periodic times for exercise

- The keeping of a spiritual journal, which might simply be your own conversation with God.

Exploring—Considering the Calls Upon Our Lives

In exploring we depend upon the Scriptures to guide us in our journey, reminded of Psalm 119:105:

**"Your word is a lamp to my feet
and a light to my path."**

Here we consider other calls; we name other gifts; we consider other possibilities. We depend upon the illumination of the Holy Spirit to guide us into the truth (John 16:13). We share our discernments about gifts, rooted in Scripture and reflected upon in the silence, with a trusted friend or two. We listen with openness to their questions, and we consider suggestions as other options to be taken seriously.

Improving and Weighing—
Discerning the Gift

The identification of our spiritual gift is improved and weighed as we continue a rigorous self-examination. We reflect on our comfort level with the process thus far. We evaluate how seriously we have taken the disciplines of Scripture study and solitude. We listen again for the voice of God and to the words of trusted friends. We acknowledge our own capacity for self-deception.

At this point we practice the scriptural admonition from 1 John 4:1:

"Beloved, do not believe every spirit, but test the spirits, to see whether they are from God."

Danny Morris and Chuck Olsen list several practices that can be adapted here. A helpful discernment practice might be to take the questions from the Spiritual Exercises from Ignatius, as appropriated by the Jesuits:

- **Does the identification of _____ as my primary spiritual gift lead me to a sense of peace, freedom, and consolation? Am I excited and energized?**

- Or does the identification of _____ as my primary spiritual gift lead me to a feeling of sadness, depression, and desolation? Am I despondent and discouraged?

The Holy Spirit, according to the Jesuit tradition, is always on the side of consolation. When God places a gift within us, there is rejoicing when that gift is discovered and released. This spiritual practice requires time for a sense of feeling to settle over a person; and this feeling also comes when an individual claims the gift and begins to move forward, at least mentally, in the direction of that gift and away from others.

At this stage, it might be helpful for the individual to seek a relationship with a spiritual director, a mentor, or a trusted friend and colleague. Here we are becoming honest with ourselves about who we are and how we are gifted, and we are also seeking accountability with someone who will help us to move toward the exercise of our gift.

Closing and Resting—Acting on Our Decision, Trusting in God

In closing we make a decision: "This is my gift!" It might be an "aha!" moment, filled with surprise. It might also be a confirmation of what we have always sensed. The word *closing* implies that a door closes, what Parker Palmer writes about when he speaks of "no way," and at the same time a door opens. At that moment we say, with the prophet Isaiah,

Here am I, Lord.

Our response to the grace of clarity about gifts is to surrender, and in that surrender we sense a trust and a peace that comes from God's presence. It is almost as if we have come home, to our true selves, when we claim the gifts that are our birthrights as Christians. And this is no less true for pastors than it is for the laity.

The Importance of the Process

The process of spiritual gift identification is important for several reasons. First, it will help the pastor to know who she is, more fully, in the context of God's mission. Second, it will also help the pastor to know how he fits into the Body of Christ that is the local congregation. Third, it will help the pastor to uncover how she is positively motivated to serve (when her gift is exercised) and how she might also be "burning out" (when her gift is neglected). And finally, in working this process the pastor will model for his congregation the importance of identifying their spiritual gifts.

The following meditation is about vocation and calling, listening and trusting.

Upright Bass

I aspired to the steadiness of the upright bass,
laying the foundation, providing the pulse.
Later I learned, or better, remembered,
that underneath are the everlasting arms
crouched over the instrument, leaning,
a shadowy figure, a mystery
birthing deep, rich sound,
an audible assurance
that it is well *(it is well . . .).*

I was not to be the bass,
but surely to know that beneath,
below, at the bottom
there was a constancy, a steadfastness,
and that in its melody, I was safe and secure
from all alarms.

My calling was not to play the bass
but to hear it, and in the hearing
my own vocation is clearly voiced:
to fly away, fly away, fly away
(in the morning . . .).
To trust is to improvise,
and to improvise is to know
the pattern well enough to depart from it,
and then to return.

—K. H. C.

CHAPTER SIX

Spiritual Gifts:
Some Words of Caution

Now concerning spiritual gifts, brothers and sisters, I do not want you to be misinformed.
(1 Corinthians 12:1)

Spiritual gifts can be abused in many ways. . . .
Some who are fully aware of the potential of spiritual gifts use them for acquiring power, gaining wealth, taking advantage or exploiting fellow believers.
(*Peter Wagner,* Your Spiritual Gifts Can Help Your Church Grow)

This seems to be the appropriate time to offer some words of caution about spiritual gifts. There are dangers associated with language about spiritual gifts and the actual expression of them. Each is present in the biblical references to gifts; in fact, the New Testament letters were written in part in response to misunderstandings about gifts.

The language of spiritual gifts is integral to the New Testament, as we have seen. As Gordon Fee has noted in *Paul, the Spirit, and the People of God,* to experience salvation in the early church was to become incorporated into the Body of Christ, the church. And this experience of salvation came to be expressed in normal and natural ways through the expression of spiritual gifts. As we learn more about spiritual gifts, and as we become acquainted with ways to order the lives of congregations around them, we find ourselves becoming more like the churches of the New Testament.

Which is, in fact, both a blessing and a curse!

Great power is unleashed in the gifts of the spirit. Congregations come alive. People discover their true callings. Those in need are touched with grace and hope. We begin to look like the church of Jesus Christ. This is the great blessing of spiritual gifts. But there is curse as well, and it is helpful to pause and consider the varied ways gifts can be misused, abused, or neglected.

There are four paths that we will want to avoid, and all are present in the New Testament churches: **gift denial, gift exaltation, gift projection**, and **gift suppression**.

Gift Denial: When I Refuse to Share My Gift

In his spiritual classic, *Life of the Beloved*, Henri Nouwen writes, *"Over the years, I have come to realize that the greatest trap in our life is not success, popularity or power, but self-rejection."*[1] When we reject ourselves, we deny God's gifts. When we reject ourselves, the image of God is diminished in us. When we reject ourselves, we resist God's grace. Nouwen then enters into a discussion of the relationship between arrogance and self-rejection:

> Maybe you think that you are more tempted by arrogance than by self-rejection. But isn't arrogance, in fact, the other side of self-rejection? Isn't arrogance putting yourself on a pedestal to avoid being seen as you see yourself? Isn't arrogance, in the final analysis, just another way of dealing with the feelings of worthlessness?[2]

Nouwen has been helpful to me in exploring the root causes of our tendency to deny our gifts. It is, he writes, a trap. It is a trap that clergy fall into: We do not fully share our gifts with our congregations. An African American pastor was assigned to a church that had been composed of mostly white people, but now found itself in a transitioning neighborhood. The assignment was explicit: Integrate the church. For some time the pastor proceeded, but the response was minimal; and in his heart he knew something was amiss. Finally the church hit bottom. A decision was made to serve the community, that was now mostly black. The church did not become integrated. It did become a thriving black church. The pastor, along the way, came to a more complete understanding of his gifts and his mission. He had, for good reason, been denying his gifts. When he felt the freedom to share them, which was an act of courage, the Body was strengthened.

Most pastors can identify some place along the way where they posed the question: Can I share my gifts with these people? Will they accept me as I am? It calls us to be vulnerable, to take risks. And yet the denial of our gifts is the denial of who we are, as God's created and called servants, among God's people. When we avoid being seen for who we are, the word cannot become flesh (John 1).

The laity of our congregations struggle with the same questions. Any pastor will recall conversations with potential leaders who respond to our appeals with "I really could never see myself serving in that role" or "I'm not a leader" or "I could never teach" or "My life is too full now as it is."

Sometimes a call should be weighed, and the answer is no. Not every call is right for us. Not every gift is present in every person. But there are persons within our congregations who have considerable gifts who also struggle with forms of low self-esteem or pride or self-rejection.

Sometimes we dig a hole in the ground and bury our talents (Matthew 25:14-30). The mission of God is not accomplished when the gifts of God are denied, hidden, and buried. And the gift of God that is each person does not flourish, blossom, and grow.

Gift Exaltation:
My Gift Is More Important Than Yours

Nouwen suggests that low self-esteem may express itself, paradoxically, in the form of arrogance. Arrogance is the root cause of *gift exaltation,* a term used by Peter Wagner of Fuller Theological Seminary. In gift exaltation we place one gift above others in significance or importance. This is again a subtle trap for pastors and churches.

It is easy enough to read the Corinthian correspondence and discover the practice of gift exaltation. Some thought they were spiritually superior to others. Some exalted the gift of glossalalia, speaking in tongues (see 1 Corinthians 12–14). Our temptation as pastors of mainline churches is to see forms of pride in these communities of faith and wonder about the errors of their ways.

But we can also be led astray. In an era of membership decline, the mainline church can easily exalt one of the spiritual gifts, such as evangelism or leadership. These gifts seem to be present among those who are identified with growing churches. Therefore, denominational officials invite pastors with these particular gifts and say, in essence, "these are the most important gifts in our time." There is always a context for gift exaltation, and while the gifts of evangelism and leadership are necessary to the healthy functioning of the Body, not every pastor has them. And a part of lowering clergy morale may be due to a reinforced message that certain gifts—shepherding, mercy, hospitality, faith—are not as significant as others, ones that can be linked more visibly to the growth and expansion of the Kingdom. As Paul writes, *"the members of the body that seem to be weaker are indispensable"* (1 Corinthians 12:22).

Gift Projection:
Why You Should Have the Gift That I Have

Gift projection is closely aligned to gift exaltation. Peter Wagner is correct in noting that this form of abuse leads Christians to feelings of guilt;[3] because we do not serve or witness in a certain way or within a particular ministry, we feel inferior. When we project gifts onto others, we are saying, *"if you were a real Christian, you would see it my way."* Leaders are prone to the mistake of gift projection: We naturally draw others into our circles, and they see the visions that we cast for them. In subtle ways we are then tempted to project our gifts onto them, and here there is resistance. In part, the resistance is an important source of feedback: Folks are sometimes telling us that we have not understood them or their gifts.[4]

Gift projection occurs in every conceivable sphere of God's kingdom: Parents impose gifts and callings onto their children. Pastors impose gifts that were present in the last congregation onto leaders in the present congregation. Laity who were blessed by a gift of the last pastor long for that in her successor. Bishops, who have excelled in some area of the Christian life, are especially perceptive to those who share their own gifts. In multiple staffs, we are tempted to hire or call individuals who have our own gifts, when the congregation might actually benefit from a more diverse staff.

We praise those who possess and exercise our gifts. We neglect or misunderstand those who have gifts that are foreign to our experiences. The fundamental problem with gift projection is stated by Paul in the form of a question: *"If all were a single member, where would the body be?"* (1 Corinthians 12:19).

Projection is the enemy of diversity. And while we say we support diversity, in a variety of contexts, it is always a struggle for us. This is true in the area of spiritual gifts.

For this reason a thorough acquaintance with the classic texts related to spiritual gifts is essential, especially 1 Corinthians 12–14 and Romans 12.

Gift Suppression: When We Attempt to Control the Gifts of Others

Because of the chaotic nature of spiritual gifts, we may be inclined to avoid the whole matter. There were problems in the church at Corinth related to spiritual gifts. There is the potential for similar problems in our own churches. When we begin to use the language of spiritual gifts, we are moving away from other models of ministry. Some of those models are more hierarchical. In the New Testament there is a movement from the dynamic and organic model of the church as the Body of Christ, seen in 1 Corinthians, to the church as it is understood in the pastoral epistles, 1 and 2 Timothy and Titus. As Gilbert Bilezikian, theologian and mentor to Bill Hybels of the Willow Creek Community Church has noted:

> Turning to the pastoral epistles (from the earlier letters of Paul) is like being transported into a different world. Suddenly, the presence of overseers, elders and deacons becomes massive and unavoidably manifest (1 Timothy 3:1-13; 5:17-22; Titus 1:5-9). Leaders suddenly march out of the shadows and stand at center stage.[5]

Suppression of gifts can be the attempt to control those gifts through church order or within congregational structures. There will be times to evaluate the appropriateness of a particular spiritual gift in an area of ministry. But the opposite danger should also be heeded: One reason for the demise of the church's mission in our culture may be the suppression of our gifts, in the context of clericalism, professionalism, and credentials.

The Gifts in the Early Church:
Three Snapshots

We have two daughters. I have shared the following with other parents, some of whom have three or more children: It is often true that we have a tremendous historical record of our first child; of the second child we have a few pictures; the third. . . . what does that third child look like?

I want to focus on three portraits, three images of the early church, of those first followers of Jesus. The first one is found in the first chapter of Acts and has to do with the question of who will be the successor to Judas, who had betrayed Jesus. They selected two who had known Jesus; they prayed for God's guidance and direction; "and they cast lots for them, and the lot fell on Matthias, and he was added to the eleven apostles" (Acts 1:12-26).

The interesting thing about this passage is that it comes between two rather amazing experiences in the early church: the ascension of Jesus, where Jesus goes up to be with the Father, and the day of Pentecost, where everyone knows a miraculous presence of the Holy Spirit. This passage is like a valley between two mountains, but it must have held some importance for Luke and has an importance for us: Church is not always about amazing, miraculous encounters with the Lord; it is sometimes about who will be the leader, who will take someone else's place, who will serve.[6]

The second picture, the second image of the early church, is one of the most powerful descriptions of community in the Bible or in any kind of writing. The followers of Jesus are together; and they devote themselves to the apostles' teaching and to prayers, to the breaking of bread and to the fellowship. They share everything they have with one another. And their community is blessed by the addition of new persons who want to experience this new life. Luke writes, *"awe came upon everyone"* (Acts 2:43). When the gifts of God are shared with the people of God, the church is awesome!

The third picture of the early church is found in Acts 5. It is a striking story, a bizarre episode in the life of the early church. If I had been writing the account of how the first church was formed, I would have left it out. It is the story of Ananias and Sapphira. Very simply, they were a part of a community that shared deeply and fully with one another; and within that context they sold a piece of property and gave only a portion to the apostles, withholding the remainder for themselves. When Peter confronted them about this, they both "fell down and died"! (Acts 5:5, 10).

This is quite a remarkable experience. I had read this passage and always dismissed it or skipped over it or thought, "that's pretty strange," until I saw the connection between Acts 2 and Acts 5. Acts 2 is about *awe*; Acts 5 is about *fear*. Acts 2 is about sharing gifts; Acts 5 is about withholding gifts. Acts 2 is about sacrifice; Acts 5 is about selfishness. Acts 2 is about abundance; Acts 5 is about scarcity. Acts 2 is about life; Acts 5 is about death. Acts 2 is a family picture that we love to show off, have framed, place above the mantel. Acts 5 is the picture that we would like to tear up and throw away. Acts 2 is human nature at its best. Acts 5 is human nature at its worst. Acts 2 is about trust and obedience. Acts 5 is about deception and faithlessness.

It is not true that the early church was a kind of "pure form" of church life in which all shared their gifts. The early church had its share of struggle and victory. It struggled between being an Acts 2 church and an Acts 5 church. We have that same struggle, as a church and as individuals. I once asked a Sunday school class how they felt reading and hearing about the experience of Acts 2:

They mentioned joy, community, sharing, fellowship, growth, laughter. I later asked how they felt hearing about the experience of Acts 5: They mentioned sadness, deception, disappointment, regret. There's something awesome about the church of Acts 2; there's nothing awesome about the church of Acts 5.

Our gift to our communities and to the world will be to create Acts 2 churches. Our gift to our children will be to create Acts 2 churches. Our gift to God will be to create an Acts 2 church. Our gift to ourselves will be to create an Acts 2 church. And if we can create such churches, Acts 2 churches, we will learn the skills to live as Acts 2 people: people who study, who praise God, who share deeply with friends, who have plenty for themselves and plenty for others, who know God's abundance and share their gifts out of that abundance.

I want you to create a mental picture in your mind of a church that is alive, a church that is joyful, a church that shares its gifts, a church that has no needy people, and a church that always has enough. That is the picture I have in my mind for my church and your church—not an Acts 5 church, an Acts 2 church, an awesome church.

There is good news. God blesses us and the church with spiritual gifts.

If I Open My Hands to Give

If I open my hands to give,
I discover that I am also receiving.

If I close my hands to possess,
I realize that I have nothing.

Jesus talked about spiritual poverty and blessedness.

Saint Francis prayed, "It is in giving that we receive."

John Wesley preached, "Make all you can, save all you can,
give all you can."

When I am following Jesus,
I experience the abundant life.
It is not exactly clear if I am the giver
or the recipient,
and it doesn't really matter:
Life is an everflowing stream,
giving becomes receiving,
grace calls forth gratitude.

—K. H. C.

CHAPTER SEVEN

Teaching Sermons on Spiritual Gifts

The word of God is living and active.
(Hebrews 4:12)

Preaching . . . is a process of transformation for
both preacher and congregation alike, as the ordi-
nary details of their everyday lives are translated
into the extraordinary elements of God's ongoing
creation.
(Barbara Brown Taylor, The Preaching Life*)*

The Eighth Day of Creation
(2 Corinthians 5)

If anyone is in Christ, there is a new creation:
everything old has passed away; see, everything
has become new! (v. 17)

I want to begin to help us to focus in these messages on the spiritual gifts that have been given to each of us as Christians. God has created each of us as unique individuals, and has placed within us gifts that can bless the lives of others and lead to our own fulfillment and joy. Let us pray: *Come Holy Spirit, fill the hearts of your faithful, and kindle in us the fire of your love. Send forth your spirit and we shall be created, and you shall renew the face of the earth. Amen.*

As we begin this journey, we acknowledge both the creative power of God to work within and among us, and also God's need for our creativity and our gifts. A few years ago there was a popular book entitled *Your God Is Too Small* by J. B. Phillips; some time after that I heard William Sloane Coffin of the Riverside Church preach a sermon entitled "Your God Is Too Big!" What were they saying? One was saying that we sometimes limit God's power or presence in the world; *we imagine that we have to do it all.* The other was making the opposite point: Sometimes we assume, because of the power and might of God, that we have to do nothing; and we become passive, we withdraw.

Who was right? My sense is that they were both correct. We *are* the new creation of God—the old has passed away, the new has come—and we have been given a share of God's restoring, reconciling ministry in the world. God is powerful, wondrous, amazing; and God's gifts, *channeled through us,* are also powerful, wondrous, amazing.[1]

Creation Is a Process

We are the new creation. We affirm the truth of Scripture, a selection that has several meanings. First, **creation is a process**, sometimes a slow one; and we who are called to be the new creation must *trust the process.* God is at work in us, changing us, slowly, sometimes imperceptibly. A Christian commented on this experience with these words. She wrote:

> At the beginning of our journey in the Christian life many of us were converted and entered a period of profound hope and excitement over the new life opening before us. We felt we were saved, we knew we had changed, and we were profoundly grateful for this gift. We understood what it meant to be in the world but not of it. We had left behind some of the alienating, death-dealing patterns that mar the world; and we lived with a new knowledge of the possibilities of the new creation.

We hoped to be faithful to a new vision of life; but as the years passed, if we were honest, we were forced to admit that we had not changed as profoundly as we had once believed. Perhaps we were often fearful; perhaps we were envious or covetous, or were troubled with a persistent, irrational anger . . . although we initially blamed others for these behaviors, we eventually acknowledged that they were a part of our personalities. As we recognized these persistent patterns, we realized that we were still deeply part of the alienated and broken dimensions of the world.[2]

Sometimes we look at ourselves and there seems nothing new about us, nothing transformative about who we are. *There does not seem to be a new creation.* But we should not be discouraged; creation is a slow process. I'm reminded of the bumper sticker: "Please be patient! God is not finished with me yet!" Patience is listed by Paul as a fruit of the spirit (Galatians 5:22), and we are called to trust God, believing that God is creating something in this world through individuals like you and me.

New Creation Takes Time

Second, in the process of new creation we must **make time for God.** Anything that is truly creative takes time. How long does it take to learn to play the piano like Bill Evans or the guitar like Doc Watson? How long does it take a Michael Jordan to master the art of basketball, or Greg Maddux to master the art of pitching, or Yo Yo Ma the cello, or Wynton Marsalis the trumpet, or Alison Kraus the fiddle? Perhaps you have embarked on a new passion: watercoloring, calligraphy, ballroom dancing, fly fishing. If so, you will admit that progress, much less perfection, does not happen overnight.

Creativity requires time set aside for practice, for devotion to the art, whether that is gymnastics or dance or piano or baseball or prayer. The new creation comes about as we *make time* for God through worship, through study, through prayer, through action. We will become new creatures as we study the Bible, as we build Habitat Houses, as we take a gift to first-time guests who join us in worship, as we pray in silence before God at the beginning or the end of the day. Will it happen instantaneously? Probably not. But we will be in the process of becoming the new creation as we make time for God.

New Creation Is Painful

Third, in the process of new creation **we must *face our pain.*** New creation means change, and change is always painful. The scripture declares that *"the old has passed away, and the new has come."* There's something profound, something therapeutic, about that statement. When we come to grips with our pain, with our losses, with our crises, only then can the old pass away; only then does the new come. And only then do we grow.

When I was a teenager, I grew almost six inches during one spring and summer. I remember waking up in the mornings and feeling a soreness in my ligaments. I was growing, and it was painful. And that's the way it often happens with us in this life. For that reason we often resist change. I was in a workshop once with a leader who remarked: *"I love change; I love it when other people change."* But God calls us to change, to grow, to be the new creation.

"Melt Me, Mold Me, Fill Me, Use Me"

Finally, as the new creation **we allow God to melt us, to mold us, to fill us, to use us,** in the words of the hymn.[3] This means that we must *be flexible,* like a piece of clay, and know that God is creating something wonderful in us. Perhaps we can allow the words of another hymn to guide us: "Have Thine Own Way, Lord!"[4] Or we can express it another way: We are called to "surrender our lives to Jesus Christ," knowing that he can do far more with them than we can. At the close of the third chapter of Ephesians, there is a wonderful benediction that captures this truth. Do you know it?

> Now to him who by the power at work within us is able to accomplish abundantly far more than all we can ask or imagine, to him be glory in the church and in Christ Jesus to all generations, forever and ever. Amen. (3:20, 21)

Augustine once observed that "God is always trying to give good things to us, but our hands are too full to receive them!"[5]

The new creation is God's work in us. But, as God's new creation, we are also becoming involved in the ongoing task of God's work in the world. In the beautiful phrase of Elizabeth O'Connor, we live in "The Eighth Day of Creation."[6] We have a role in the creation of our children, in the creation of our workplaces, in the creation of our homes, in the creation of this congregation, in the creation of our community.

New creation happens as we trust the process . . . as we make time for God . . . as we face our pain . . . and as we allow God to *shape, mold, fill and use* us. God is the master potter, and God wants to do something wonderful in the life of every Christian. It is called the new creation. When there is new creation, the old passes away and the new appears. This is the promise of God for us. Believe the good news! You are a part of the new creation. Amen.

Why Can't Everyone Be More Like Me? (1 Corinthians 12)

> *Indeed, the body does not consist of one member*
> *but of many.*   (v. 14)

We are focusing during these messages on the spiritual gifts that God has placed within us and across the

Christian community. In the first message we reflected on the new creation that occurs in the Christian as he or she begins to claim his or her giftedness and joins with God in the process of creation.

Paul's letters to the Corinthians were written in the middle of the first century. The primary theme of our scripture for today is how Christians can live together without splitting into factions. *"Each of you says, 'I belong to Paul' or 'I belong to Apollos' or 'I belong to Cephas,' or 'I belong to Christ'"* he reports. But then he asks: *"Has Christ been divided?"* (1:12-13).

There are problems in the Christian community at Corinth. There is bizarre sex and overwhelming greed (chapter 5). There are lawsuits against each other (chapter 6). Many of the people in our news would have felt at home in first-century Corinth!

Paul is attempting to make sense out of the gospel in a culture marked by fraud, deceit, and self-centeredness, a culture very much like our own. These Christians had heard the message of Galatians, that they were free in Christ, no longer bound by the constraints of the law, liberated to follow Jesus. But their interpretation needed correction: They understood their relationship to God as a special knowledge and privilege and as a freedom from having to live a life of integrity and faithfulness. The Corinthian Christians understood freedom as freedom *to do as they pleased.* Somewhere, Paul must have felt, there had been a breakdown in communication.

How did Paul choose to respond? By using the language of gifts—gifts that God places within us, gifts that have a purpose, gifts that allow us to serve others, diverse gifts. This section of 1 Corinthians is found in chapters 12, 13, and 14. How can we read this letter from Paul and hear it as if he is speaking to us?

We Accept Our Gifts

We can accept our own gift and become comfortable with them. This is difficult for many of us. I imagine that each of us would like to be something other than who we are, in some way. I mentioned my growth spurt as a teenager during the spring and summer when I grew six inches. As a teenager what a person most wants to do is conform, to be like the others. What I wanted least to be was six to eight inches taller than almost every other person. There were times when I thought, *"Wouldn't it be great to be normal height!"*

And we have all probably said something to that effect:

I'm too tall.
I weigh too much.
I'm not smart enough.
I didn't go to the right school.
I'm not as good with my kids as that person.
I don't seem to be making it in the world like that guy.

You could add to the list. In this life's journey we are prone to neglect *who we are* in favor *of what we perceive in another person.* We are inclined to measure ourselves against others, and usually we fall short. And so **we deny the very gift, the very uniqueness of who we are!**

Jesus Christ frees us from all of that. A recent *National Geographic* had a wonderful article on the Galilee region of Israel; and someone from Tennessee, who is both a nuclear engineer and a preacher, described going into the Jordan River, "When I went into those waters, all I heard was a voice saying, 'You are my beloved child; I am pleased with you.'"[7]

Now we don't all have to go to Galilee and to the Jordan River, although it is a wonderful place—one of the most meaningful experiences in my life was the reaffirmation of my baptism as I was immersed into the waters of the Jordan—but those words are for us, for you and me, *"you are my beloved child; I am pleased with you."*

We are called to accept our own gifts, to rejoice in our own uniqueness. Each of us is created in God's image. Each of us has a gift to share with others, and that gift is not so much what we do as *who we are.* Gordon Cosby said it well: "God is gathering jewels for the eternal crown, and I am one of the jewels."[8]

We Accept and Honor the Gifts of Others

We can rejoice in our own gifts. We can also accept the gifts of others. I am convinced that we are initially attracted to people as marriage partners because of their differences, because of their uniqueness; and then we spend all of our time and energies trying to sand those rough edges and to make them more like—like us! This is really a lifetime project! That wonderful personality trait in your husband or wife that brought a smile to your face and a lump in your throat and a faster beat within your heart while you were dating can become an irritant, a thorn in the flesh. And deep down, we are saying under our breath, *"Why can't you be more like me?"*

We are unique, we are different, and that is precisely God's design for the church: *"God arranged the members in the body, each one of them, as he chose"* (12:18). The body is strong because each muscle, each joint, each ligament, has a different function. And where there is weakness, Paul insists, take note: The members of the body that seem to be weaker are indispensable, for God enters into the world and overcomes the world through a crucified Lord.

The Beauty of God's Design

I invite you, as a Christian, to claim your gifts, to celebrate your uniqueness. As a participant in the church, I call upon you to affirm the gifts of others, to rejoice in the diversity of gifts (12:4).

A wonderful parable expresses this truth: A person had a flower garden. And in the flower garden he planted a variety of flowers. There were tulips, which bloomed in early spring. There were roses, which bloomed in the fall until they were covered by winter snows; and around the edge there was some greenery, which had no visible bloom. It was a beautiful garden, and everyone was happy.

But one day, early in the spring, the roses and the mums and the greenery looked around, and they saw that the tulips were in full bloom—while at best they had begun to shoot forth only tiny buds. And they began to wonder: *What's wrong with us? Why aren't we blossoming forth?* The more they thought about it, the more anxious they became till frantically they tore their tender little buds open and spread their yet unformed petals apart. But there was no beauty in it. Rather than blooming, they withered and died.

In many respects, we are like flowers. Some of us bloom very early in the spring—some bloom in the middle of the summer—some bloom in late fall; and possibly some don't have any visible bloom at all, and that's okay. In fact, it's better than okay; it's good. It's the way the Master Gardener designed it.

But sometimes we look around and we see others blossoming, and we begin to wonder "What's wrong with me?" Or at other times we may have blossoms and not see those in others and wonder, "Why don't they get with it?" Each way we miss the process of creation that God is bringing forth. Each way we miss the beauty of God's design.

There is a diversity of gifts. God has designed each of us to be something unique and special. Rejoice in your uniqueness. Don't lose it. Claim it. And learn to cultivate an appreciation for the ways that others bloom.

And as we bloom and flourish, blossom and grow, God is glorified. Amen.

Can a Church Be Spiritual?
(1 Corinthians 14:1-12)

Pursue love and strive for the spiritual gifts . . .
so that the church may be built up.

(*vv. 1, 5*)

I was watching a television talk show, one of those nameless ones in the middle of a summer evening. An actress whose name I have forgotten was being interviewed. Naturally, she was an authority on a variety of subjects, and she was holding forth. The discussion turned to religion. *"I don't go to church,"* she commented, pausing for effect, *"but I am spiritual. Spirituality is very important to me."*

Somehow those words have come to mean two different things. *Spirituality* means one thing, *church* another. *Spirituality* means something good. *Church* means something bad. Would a famous actress actually admit that she went to church? Probably not. But she would claim to have a spirituality, to be a spiritual person.

These two issues—what it means to be spiritual and what it means to be the church—are at the heart of our scripture. And Paul's struggle with these issues can help us, as a gathered body of believers and as individual Christians.

Building a Church

There is an obvious concern: What to do about those folk who speak in tongues at the church in Corinth? Paul offers clear advice, laced with a practical, constructive appeal to his listeners, and it is grounded in the frequency of the word *upbuilding*. You can help me to emphasize the point. I will read portions of the chapter; and when I point to you, that is your cue to say *build up*. Here goes:

Those who prophesy *build up* other people as they speak
to them (v. 3).
No one understands those who speak in tongues,
but those who prophesy *build up* the church (v. 2).
Those who speak in a tongue *build up* themselves,
but those who prophesy *build up* the church (v. 4).
The one who prophesies is greater than the one who
speaks in tongues, unless someone interprets, so that
they may *build up* the church (v. 5).
Strive for the spiritual gifts, in order to *build up* the
church (v. 12).
When you come together, each one has a hymn, a lesson,
a revelation, a tongue, or an interpretation.
Let everything be done to *build up* the church (v. 26).

By our presence, by our gifts, we *build up* the community. I remember an elderly gentleman who attended a rural church I once served. He had been deaf for many years. Someone asked him, "Why do you still come to preaching" (as they called it)? He responded, *"I want people to know which side I'm on!"* We are to be on the side that *builds up* the church!

A Private Prayer Language or Public Speech?

Paul is teaching us, encouraging us, pleading with us to *build up* the church. We can understand his appeal in another way, by listening to a more recent translation of this passage from *The Message* by Eugene Peterson. In it he translates the Greek word for *tongues* as "prayer language."

The one who prays using a private "prayer language"
certainly gets a lot out of it, but proclaiming God's

truth to the church in its common language brings the whole church into growth and strength. I want all of you to develop intimacies with God in prayer, but please don't stop with that. Go on and proclaim his dear truth to others. (1 Corinthians 14:4-5)

The spiritual life is important, Paul says, but *it is always life to be shared with others.* Our private, personal spiritual lives are essential; but isn't it wonderful when that spirit, that intimacy with God bubbles to the surface and is a blessing to others? My bishop, Charlene Kammerer, noted in a sermon once that the Holy Spirit comes most powerfully in events that are public: wind, fire, debate, audible speech, confusion.

The word Paul uses to contrast the private prayer language is *prophecy.* A prophet does not predict the future. A prophet speaks God's word in the present. A prophetic word is a word that *builds up,* that sets right, that gives insight, maybe even changes our lives.

I remember a word of prophecy from my early teenage years. I went to a church in south Georgia that had a Sunday evening service. The numbers were smaller in those services, and they were less formal. We would sing requested hymns, pray for the sick and the lost, hear a message, and often, after the closing hymn and before the benediction, the pastor would ask if there was anyone who had a word of testimony to share. Almost no one ever did. In fact, I will make a confession—as a young person I was almost hoping no one would, because we had been there awhile, and I was ready to make my way toward home. I know that with a great stretch of the imagination you can understand how I felt!

Anyway, this particular evening our pastor asked if anyone had anything on their hearts. And a man who was a respected pillar of the church spoke up. "I've got something to say," he began. "The Lord has been good enough to allow me to live for almost seventy-five years, and I have only recently come under the conviction that I have been all wrong about people who are of a different race than me. I have asked God to forgive me, and I urge anyone else here to listen to what God might be saying to them."

With those words Bob was finished. No one said a word. But Bob had spoken prophecy! And he had helped to build up the body unto its head, Jesus Christ, in whom, Paul wrote in Galatians, *"there is neither Jew nor Greek, slave nor free, male nor female"* (3:28 NIV). Bob had uttered a word that needed to be heard. That evening we were truly the church of Jesus Christ. The word of God had changed Bob's life. And something within spoke to me and said, *"If God could speak to Bob, God might speak to you; if God could change Bob's life, God might change your life!"*

Always speak a word that builds up the community. The Christian community gathers in order to share gifts with one another. We gather in our strengths and weaknesses. We come together to receive the grace of God. And yes, we come together in order that we might be fed spiritually: by one another, by the Word, by music, by prayer.

What Is Spirituality?

It is fine that we have private, personal experiences with God. For each of the past eight years I have taken at least one personal, private, silent retreat of two to three days. In saying this I am not boasting—I'm saying that I value the private prayer language of the heart of which Paul speaks. I do not speak in tongues, but I believe that communion with Jesus Christ is being drawn more and more into a dynamic, living relationship with him.

But there is more to the Christian life than personal spirituality. There is the church. I say this not because I happen to be the pastor of a church. I believe that God has designed the Christian life to be lived in community.

In his book, *Paul, the Spirit and the People of God*, Gordon Fee poses this scene:

> A single person is sitting at home in front of the TV; a Christian broadcast is on, a sermon is preached, an invitation is given, and the person responds by "accepting Christ." But the only "church" the person attends is by way of the TV, with no connection to a local body of believers. The question: Is this person saved? I would answer: Only God knows, but such salvation lies totally outside the New Testament frame of reference.[9]

God's design for the Christian faith is that we live it together. Every time you share with me, every time I encourage you, every time you forgive another person, every time you allow yourself to receive love or grace from someone else, the church is being built up. We cannot do it alone. We need God, and we need each other.

Can a church be spiritual? If we can truly make love the guiding principle of all that we do, if we can seek to know and share our gifts, if we can build up one another —then we are a spiritual body, and then we are truly the church of Jesus Christ. Gordon Fee again says it well:

> "To be saved," in the Pauline view, means to become part of the *people* of God, who by the Spirit are born into God's *family* and therefore joined to one another as one *body*. . . . God is not simply saving diverse individuals and preparing them for heaven; rather he is creating a *people* for his name, among whom God can dwell and who in their life *together* will reproduce God's life and character in all its unity and diversity.[10]

Strive for the spiritual gifts, to build up the church! Let everything be done to build up the church. Amen.

You Are a Gift From God
(1 Timothy 4)

Do not neglect the gift that is in you. . . . Pay
close attention to yourself, and to your teaching;

> *continue in these things, for in so doing this you*
> *will save both yourself and your hearers.*
>
> *(vv. 14, 16)*

Elizabeth O'Connor tells the story about Michelangelo's pushing a huge rock down a street. A curious neighbor sitting lazily on the porch of his house called to him and inquired why he labored so over an old piece of stone. Michelangelo is reported to have answered, "Because there is an angel in that rock that wants to get out!"[11] This morning's scripture speaks to this truth. "Do not neglect the gift that is in you" Timothy is told. He has been given a gift, in his case the gift to teach, and this inner knowledge has been confirmed by the outward act of the laying on of hands. Now, the scripture tells us, he is not to neglect the gift, to leave it buried within, to hide it under a bushel.

Timothy had a gift. And it is my conviction that every Christian has a gift, and the word for us in this scripture also might be not to neglect the gift that is within us. We are instead to use our gifts, to exercise them, to share them with others.

I want to look briefly at this passage of scripture with two questions in mind. First, *Why do we neglect our gifts?* And second, *How can we ensure that we will not neglect them but live fully and creatively, abundantly and faithfully as God's gifted people?*

The Denial of Our Gifts

First, we have a tendency to neglect or deny our gifts because we think too little of them. This must have been an issue for Timothy. *"What do I have to share with these people who have so much more age and wisdom than I?"* he might have been thinking. *"Don't let anyone put you down because you're young,"* the writer says to him.

We often neglect or deny our gifts because of feelings of inferiority or low self-esteem. *"Does God really want to use me?"* we ask. *"Does God want to accomplish something through me?"* The answer, based on the kinds of people that we read about in the Bible, is probably yes.

God calls Moses; Moses says, "I'm slow of speech." God calls Paul; Paul confesses that he does not possess "eloquent wisdom." But later, in one of his letters, he had the wonderful insight that we have the treasure of the gospel in earthen vessels (2 Corinthians 4:7 RSV), to let everyone know that the power belongs to God and not to us!

God wants to use ordinary people like you and me. Who else would God choose to use? God did not enter human history through kings and emperors and rulers; God came in the form of a baby, born in a cattle stall, the child of Mary and Joseph. God can work through you; God can use you; don't neglect your gift!

Strategies to Unleash Our Giftedness

But how do we keep that from happening? We all know people who are surely gifted and yet have not "unleashed" the power of God's presence and love in them. Let me offer three suggestions.

First, **we can live in dialogue with Scripture.** Listen to this recent translation of another passage from the Timothy letters: "Every part of Scripture is God-breathed and useful one way or another—showing us truth, exposing our rebellion, correcting our mistakes, training us to live God's way. Through the Word we are put together and shaped up for the tasks God has for us." (2 Timothy 3:16-17 *Message*).

All Scripture is inspired—which means "God-breathed." It is no accident that breath and spirit are so closely connected in the Scriptures. God breathes into us and creates us. The Scriptures breathe new life into us, and we are a new creation. In this process of creation all of the periphery, the incidentals, the baggage are taken away; and something truly wonderful appears: We are shaped for the tasks God has for us. What has been hidden is now revealed.

Second, **we can listen to our mentors in the faith**. For Timothy that person was Paul. Our mentors are encouragers, those men and women who see something in us, who see the angel in the rock, and prod us forward into the painful and wondrous work of becoming who, in God's design, we are intended to be. There is often for individuals an inner sense of who we are, of what we have been created to be; but someone has to outwardly confirm that—for Timothy that had happened in the laying on of hands.

In the Christian faith we define a sacrament as an "outward and visible sign of an inward and spiritual grace." Even when something important has happened inwardly, spiritually, we need to do something outwardly to show that the inner experience has become a reality.

Mentors do that for us. And we can do that for others. I'm speaking at a very simple level here: encourage, affirm, uplift, strengthen, and build up. In the Church of the Saviour in Washington, D.C., mentors are called "patrons of gifts," those persons who make the giftedness of others possible. In Henri Nouwen's *Life of the Beloved*, it is the difference between knowing that we have been chosen by God, and then experiencing that as a blessing from another human being! We are always blessed by the touch of another person, which says "You are special; you are beloved in the sight of God—and I believe in you." Mentors do that for us. And I hear Timothy's mentor speaking in this passage: "You can do it!"

Finally, **the use of our gifts is an issue of profound, life-altering importance for others**. As you use your gifts, Timothy says, you will save both yourself and your hearers. What a statement! As we use our gifts, we save ourselves and those affected by our gifts. Our gifts really matter to us, for our own sake. Someone has put it this way: Salvation is for creation. We are saved in order to be a blessing to others, through the particular gifts that God has placed within us. And in that process, everyone becomes closer to us.

There is an ancient story about a Rabbi named Isaac, son of Yekel, who had a dream. The dream told him to travel from Cracow to Prague and to look for a treasure under the bridge leading to the king's palace. Rabbi Isaac did not pay attention to the dream the first night, except to note it. On the second night, when he had the same dream, he became more restless. On the third night, when the same voice spoke, he sensed the urgency and arose the next morning to travel to the king's palace.

When he got to the bridge, he found that the bridge was guarded night and day. Nevertheless, he went to the bridge every morning and kept walking around until evening. Finally, the captain of the guards asked him in a kindly way if he were waiting for someone. Rabbi Isaac told him about the dream that had brought him here from a faraway city. The captain laughed! "You wore out your shoes to come here because of a dream. If I listened to dreams, I would have made a trip to Cracow and dug for treasure under the stove in a room of a Jew, Rabbi Isaac, son of Yekel. I can just imagine what that would have been like, in a city where half of the Jews are named Isaac and half are named Yekel!" And he laughed again. Rabbi Isaac bowed to the ground, turned in the direction of his own house, made the journey home, dug the treasure from under his stove, and built the House of Prayer.[12]

There is a treasure, a gift, within you.
You are a gift from God.
Do not neglect the gift that is within you.

*And in so doing you will discover salvation
for yourself and for others. Amen.*

A Provocative Church
(Hebrews 10:11-25)

> *Let us not give up meeting together, as some are
> in the habit of doing, but let us encourage one
> another.*
>
> *(v. 25 NIV)*

Jesus has paid it all, our scripture begins: "When
Christ had offered for all time a single sacrifice for sin,
'he sat down at the right hand of God.'" In his offering of
life, our lives are made whole, complete. And in Jesus we
come into a new relationship with God because God
makes a new covenant with us. God, religion, and faith
are not externals out there. The new covenant is internal,
engraved on our hearts, impressed upon our minds. This
new covenant, this new and living way, replaces the old
relationship, the old law, which we could never keep,
never live up to. There is now forgiveness, full and final
forgiveness, accomplished through the cross of Jesus.
Jesus paid it all.

Draw Near

This reality of new covenant, if we believe it, has profound implications for how we envision life. It is, in the
words of the scripture, **"a new and living way."** I want to
consider this new and living way briefly from a few different angles of vision. Verse 21 reads: "*Since we have a
great high priest, Jesus . . . let us approach with a true heart in
full assurance of faith.*"

This is a word about coming nearer to God. In the
Scriptures, especially the Psalms, we read of going *up* to
Jerusalem. It takes effort to approach God. But God

invites us to come closer. Our God is an invitational God. This is a part of the new and living way. God is not someone who wants to keep distance from us. God wants us to draw near by faith.

What does it mean for us to come into God's presence with full assurance? It is to take a step of faith. It is through the discipline of *worship*. We don't always feel like coming to worship. We don't always feel worthy of worshiping God. For that reason it is a discipline. It is something we do—worship, the work of the people—not because God needs our worship, but because we need to have our hearts lifted, our minds focused beyond ourselves, our perspectives broadened, and our souls enriched. Since we have this great high priest, Jesus, in the house of God, let us come into his presence with full assurance. We have been invited. We belong here.

Hang in There

This new and living way includes another dimension. We are to **"hold fast to the confession of our hope without wavering."** This is the call to keep at it, to hang in there. Hebrews is a letter written to a persecuted church. *"Recall the earlier days when, after you had been enlightened, you endured a hard struggle with sufferings, sometimes being publicly exposed to abuse and persecution, and sometimes being partners with those so treated"* (10:32-33). From the beginning, the church of Jesus has known persecution. In places throughout our world today, China and Cuba, Nicaragua and El Salvador, Iran and Saudi Arabia, Christians are being persecuted. This is being drawn to our attention, and it is not my intention to politicize this issue. The point is that our brothers and sisters in Christ all over the world are hearing this word of *encouragement*—hold fast to the confession of our hope without wavering—and they understand it.

The question for us: "How do we understand it? How

do we hold fast to our hope?" It is through the discipline of prayer. Prayer helps us to live by hope. Prayer helps us to believe that God is at work in the world. I heard a humorous story recently about a fellow who was building a tavern.

The church in that community got up in arms and began to pray for its demise. As things would have it, lightning struck the tavern, and it burned to the ground. The tavern owner sued the church for damages. The church responded, "What did we have to do with that?" The judge heard all of this and finally commented, "All I can say is, the tavern owner believes in prayer, and the Christians don't!"

Do we believe in prayer? Prayer is the way through the sufferings, the struggles, the senselessness of life. We pray as we claim the promises of God, as we hold fast to hope.

Provoke One Another

The new and living way, made possible by Jesus, includes a third dimension: **"Let us consider how to provoke one another to love and good deeds"** (v. 24) or "stir up" one another, as the New King James Version has it. What does it mean to provoke one another to good deeds?

We gather together to stir up one another to good deeds, to deliberate acts of kindness, as someone has expressed it. That is the purpose of the church. Now I know it is not always the way the church functions. A bishop once commented when someone called him to complain about the church that he was thankful they didn't know as much about the church as he did!

How can we reclaim the simplicity of this core value of the faith? We are here to provoke one another to good works, to stir up one another into a people who bring goodness into the world.

Come Together

We *approach* God by faith. We *hold fast* to our confession by hope. We *provoke* one another to good deeds by love. These dimensions of the new and living way form the community of Jesus, and that leads to a key insight in this passage. *"Do not neglect to meet together,"* the scripture teaches us, "as is the habit of some, but encourage one another."

Perhaps you have had the experience of grilling out, or barbecuing, as they call it in other parts of the world. The pieces of charcoal are arranged together, the flame is lit, the fire builds, and the heat increases. And then one piece of charcoal falls to the side, gets separated. And you know what happens? Left there it loses its heat; it becomes a little colder. That is the way it is with the church of Jesus. Left to ourselves, we become a little colder, a little more distant.

We made calls in one congregation, inviting folk to be in worship for Consecration Sunday. Of the multitude of calls, one went like this. The person on the other end of the line said, "I haven't been in church in over a year." Now I don't know if she was being apologetic about herself, judgmental toward the church, or simply being evasive for one reason or another. Whatever the circumstance, this is not God's design for a person who has been made a part of the new covenant.

The good news is that when that piece of coal is placed back with the others, the fire builds once again within it, the heat increases, the fire builds, and the coal begins to generate heat. We were created to generate heat, to build a fire, to spread good news, to fan the flames that would increase the light of the world within ourselves and among others.

How can we light the fire? Some practical suggestions:

1. We can encourage each other with our words. Words

are powerful. They have either life-giving or demonic power. By the words that we speak to one another we can provide an uplift. And the uplift can be the breath that literally fans the flame, that stirs someone to do something that is significant.

2. We can empower the mission of Jesus through our gifts. God works through human beings, and the mission of Jesus happens whenever a gift is shared in some tangible way. Our gifts can be the kindling that ignites a movement. Emil Brunner once remarked, "The church exists for mission as a fire exists for burning." What gift of love can you offer? It may seem small, but remember the words of the chorus: *"It only takes a spark to get a fire going."*

3. We can enrich the life of another person through our presence. You may wake up on a Sunday morning and think, "I'm not really into it today. The house is a mess or the week has been chaos or I'm not fit to be around anyone." But consider: Your purpose in being in worship or Sunday school might be to enrich the life of someone else. The fire might be lit through your presence.

Do not neglect to meet together but encourage each other, "and all the more as you see the Day approaching." The day of salvation is coming, when Christ will live and reign among us. There is an urgency about the faith. We are called to respond today, this day, the very day in which we live.

- May God give you the gift of faith, that your worship might be offered to God.
- May God give you the gift of hope, that you may persevere in prayer.
- May God give you the gift of love, that you may encourage, provoke, stir up one another

to light a fire in this world, a fire that will make us whole.

Do not neglect to meet together. I close with a passage from Dietrich Bonhoeffer, a German Christian who was put to death by the Gestapo in 1945. It is about our life together:

> It is easily forgotten that the fellowship of Christian [brothers and sisters] is a gift of grace, a gift of the Kingdom of God that any day may be taken from us, that the time that still separates us from utter loneliness may be brief indeed. Therefore, let [the one] who until now has had the privilege of living a common Christian life with other Christians praise God's grace from the bottom of his heart. Let him thank God on his knees and declare: It is grace, nothing but grace, that we are allowed to live in community with Christian [brothers and sisters].[13]

Different Gifts, One Purpose (Romans 12:3-5)

I want to explore four invitations to enter fully into the Christian life, within the context of Romans 12. These invitations are very simple. Each builds on the one that comes before it.

First, **claim your gift.** God has made you in a particular way, given you a definite shape. Claim that. Don't try to be someone you're not. Eugene Peterson translates our passage from Romans in *The Message:* "Let's just go ahead and be what we were made to be." You were created in the image of God (Genesis 1). We begin to enter into the Christian life as we begin to lay claim to our giftedness.

This takes some trial and error. It takes some faith. It involves taking a risk. It flows out of a belief in God's grace, which is operative in our lives. It is foundational: claiming our gifts. In writing we might call it "finding our voice"; in basketball "knowing where our shot is on the court"; in the world of work it is knowing our strengths and our limitations.

We all have strengths. And we all have a gift to claim. The obstacle to claiming our giftedness is *comparing ourselves with others*. Again, Eugene Peterson's translation is helpful. *"Let's just go ahead and be what we were made to be, without enviously or pridefully comparing ourselves with each other, or trying to be something we aren't."* I want to share with you a reflection on comparison by Jim Jackson, a United Methodist pastor who lives in Houston, Texas. He says it well:

> We would all be happier if we could find a way to stop comparing ourselves with others. Comparisons are the basis of much discontent and poor self-esteem. The comparisons we make cause us to compete with each other. Competition makes life stressful, and it shatters community. It's hard to be peaceful when you are competing. And it is hard to be a friend when you are competing.
>
> Competition begins early in life. We are asked to compete against *each* other in grades, in sports, and in appearance. We spend our lives measuring ourselves against others professionally, financially, educationally, physically, emotionally, relationally, and even spiritually. When we win, we feel good about ourselves. When we underperform, we feel bad about ourselves. I believe it is cruel and unjust for us to compare ourselves with anyone else. Why? Five reasons come to mind.
>
> First, we are all different. It is a scientific fact that you are not like anyone else who has ever lived. Look at your fingerprint, and then look at the fingerprint of the person next to you. They are different. We are all different.

Second, we all have different strengths and weaknesses. In this congregation we have people who are gourmet cooks, and professional musicians, and award winning teachers, and winning gymnasts, and talented artists, and amazing photographers, and I could go on. We have more than our share of strengths. We also have our share of weaknesses. Any community of at least one person does. Do I need to make a list?

Third, no matter how good I might be at something, there is someone who will do it better on a given day. It is easy to get demoralized when we compare ourselves at our worst to others at their best.

Fourth, the people who seem to be heroes in our society always stand on the shoulders of others. We often see the end result, the public act. We don't see all that's going on behind the scenes to make something truly significant happen.

Fifth, comparisons do not go to the heart of the matter. It is possible to be better than someone else and yet still be operating far below your potential. Conversely, it is possible to be less proficient than others and be living up to your highest potential. The real issue is not how you are doing in comparison to others, but whether or not you are doing your best."[14]

Comparing ourselves with others is an obstacle to claiming our gift. We can overcome this obstacle if we remember a simple affirmation: *I am a gift from God.*

A second invitation to enter fully into the Christian life: **Honor the gifts of others.** There is an additional obstacle to entering fully into the Christian life, and this one keeps us from honoring the gifts of others. I'm talking about *projection*, which is the *experience* of forcing others to be like us. This is easy for pastors to do. It is easy for congregations to do. It is easy for parents to do. It is easy for spouses to do. You know you are at a certain stage in marriage when your spouse leaves self-help magazines open to certain pages, or when you think about enrolling your spouse in a class. When we do this we take the role, the place of God. Remember the statement "God loves you and has a wonderful *plan* for your life." Sometimes we take the role of God. We say, maybe not verbally, but we say it anyway, "I'm your husband/wife, I'm your boss or mother or father, and I have a wonderful plan for your life." I'm stretching the point, but only a little.

We can learn to honor the gifts of others if we unlearn this temptation to project onto others. And this temptation, to *project*, is rooted in our not fully believing in the importance, uniqueness, potential of our own gifts.

Let me show you "a more excellent way." We can begin to honor the gifts of others. This is the word for us from the apostle Paul in Romans: Some are prophets and give new life and new vision to others; some are generous in their giving; some are effective in their leading; some are compassionate in their relationships with others; some are helpful in their teaching. One of the ways we can do that is to say these simple words each day: *You are different from me, and that's good!*

A third invitation: **Discover a mission in life.** Once we have claimed our giftedness, and once we know and begin to practice the honoring of the gifts of others, we are on the way to a third dimension of the Christian life. *Each of us* is here, on this planet, to discover a mission in life. You might use a different word to describe what I am calling your mission. Richard Bolles, who is as helpful as any writer I know on career planning, gives us a list of words: *my goal, my target, my purpose, my objective, my plan, my aim, my intention, my design, my ambition.*[15]

This is the "why" question. "Why" am I here? I like a couple of the words for mission: *goal* and *aim*. Our lives, I believe, have a true purpose, a true goal, a true aim; and when we are using our gifts, we are heading toward our goal. When we are not using our gifts, we do not have a correct aim; and the result is that we "miss the mark." This is one of the meanings of sin, to miss the mark. When we are not about the mission God has for us in the world, we are missing the mark; we are "living in sin."

To lay claim to your gifts, to discover your mission in life, is one of the purest forms of a Christian life. It is to live in that place where worship becomes service. What is your mission? How can you discover it?

A fourth word: We are called to **unite in a common mission** within Christ's Body, with each person's gift complementing the others. Each gift, each voice, is needed. Instead of comparing ourselves to each other, we help each other, we encourage each other. One of my concerns for the church is that we have a very clear sense of what our mission is: to grow spiritually, to form an expanding circle of acceptance and love, to share our gifts and creativity, and to serve Jesus Christ as we reach out to others. That is a mission that cannot be achieved by one person. It is a common mission. It is a mission that calls forth all our gifts. And, I believe, as we find ourselves fulfilling this mission, as a congregation, we will be teaching individuals within the congregation to discover and fulfil their own missions in life.

How I've Changed My Mind About the Ministry (Ephesians 4)

To equip the saints for the work of ministry.
(Ephesians 4:12)

I am a big basketball fan. Although I am no longer invited to "young adult" gatherings, I occasionally play. And I always know something is different the next morning when I wake up and struggle to get out of bed. I'm not a teenager anymore. I have a favorite college team, Duke, although I would never stoop to using the pulpit to disclose who that is; but as a kid I also had a favorite pro team, the Boston Celtics. A few years ago, at the end of their dynasty, the Celtics were playing the Chicago Bulls, who happened to be at the beginning of their reign. The game was close. A brilliant young Chicago player named Michael Jordan had scored sixty-two points—phenomenal—but the Celtics had won. After the game a reporter had asked Robert Parrish, whose nickname is "the Chief," for a comment about his performance. He responded: *"It's hard for one person to win a basketball game."*

I want to share with you a pattern for ministry that I am only recently beginning to accept, to feel comfortable with: *What I do with others, what I give to others, is more important that what I do myself.* I have served churches where everything revolved around me. The problem, of course, is that I am no longer serving those churches: I am here, in my present ministry. There must be a different way to go about it.

The pattern is laid out for us in the Scripture: The gifts God gave are that some would be apostles, some prophets, some pastors and teachers, to equip the saints, or "to train Christians" (Ephesians 4:12 *Message)* for the work of ministry or for the task of servanthood. This is happening in the church. This takes the focus off me and puts it on all of us, as God's people. We are a team, a team with a mission. This mission takes us into the exciting and dangerous world of spiritual gifts. We might play different positions with different intensities at different times; but we are called to be on this mission team, to use *all* of the gifts of all of God's people. It is very difficult to achieve any kind of success when we use the gifts of only one person, or even a few. *"How has my mind changed about the ministry?"* A first shift came when I realized that the ministry does not belong to me; it belongs to all of us. If I were to sum up this shift in a word, it would have only two letters: *us.*

As a young adult I had a real passion for wanting people to come to faith in Jesus Christ through a personal relationship with him. I was involved in witnessing in some pretty direct ways to those close to me and to total strangers. At times I was spiritually arrogant. I have asked God to forgive me for some of the ways I interacted with people. And I have come to discover that a core piece of the evangelical task is to call people to *maturity* in Jesus Christ. The equipping of the saints is for the maturing of the Body of Christ so that we are no longer tossed back and forth getting tripped up by trivialities— so that we can speak the truth in love to one another, so that we can grow up into Jesus Christ who is the head of the Body, the church.

Those are key words for me: *grow up*. Sometimes we as a church are simply called to grow up! Now, we know how to do this with children. We expect children to progress, to discover their identities, to blossom and flourish; and then, Bill Cosby would say, we expect them to leave. How does the church grow up? It becomes more like Jesus, whose roots were sunk deeply in prayer, whose life was invested profoundly in the calling of disciples, whose heart was with the last, the least, and the lost. This is our mission too, the mission of Jesus.

Paul is focusing on growth, the church growing up into Jesus. With children, we would say we focus on their strengths and on what they do that is positive, and we call that forth. And that has been a learning for me in the church. I will not focus, dwell on, become obsessed with what is wrong. I will not avoid occasions of conflict. But my focus will be on the signs of life and health, on the individuals and groups that are being led into the mission of Jesus that is within our congregation and beyond it, on those persons who are joining and being knit together, promoting the growth of the Body, building it up in love.

Early in the ministry I focused almost all of my attention on the pathology that was present in the church, in other people, and in me. Then I discovered that I could be most helpful to people if I helped to create a community that was becoming more Christlike, a Body that was stronger, a people in love with each other and God. That is what we need. This can be our work together.

And so, a second word for us would be almost as simple as the first one. We are called to grow up into Jesus Christ, who is our head.

A shifting pattern of ministry: It belongs to all of us (the first third of Ephesians 4), then a focus on growth and maturity (the middle third of Ephesians 4), and finally (in the latter third of Ephesians 4) a continuing need for conversion.

I can remember a time and place when I gave my heart and life to Jesus. I was attending a campus student group, and the guest leader was talking about the importance of reading the Bible each day. I felt touched, convicted, through his words, which were very simple. It was a conversion. It was a call to leave behind the old life and to enter into the new world. That was more than twenty years ago. Since then I have had other conversions. Why? Because, you see, it is very difficult to leave the old life behind. God is not finished with me.

Conversion is the difficult work of God within us, and we resist it. Someone has described it this way: When you ask God into your life, you think he is going to come into your spiritual house, look around, and see that you need a new floor or better furniture, and that everything needs just a little cleaning; and so you go along for the first six months thinking how nice life is now that God is there. Then you look out the window one day and see that there is a wrecking ball outside. It turns out that God thinks the whole foundation is shot, and you are going to have to start over from scratch.[16]

In the first half of the letter of Ephesians, we read about all that God has done for us, through grace, the magnificent gift of God that we do not earn, that we do not deserve, that we cannot repay. The experience of grace, which is an experience of continuing conversion, is our invitation into the new life. And the new life is described in all too specific language in the latter portion of this fourth chapter of Ephesians:

- Put away your former way of life, your obsessions with sex and money, which had taken the place of God;

- Be renewed, live faithfully, be holy, which is to say, live differently than the world;

- Speak the truth but in a way that shows love for others; be honest, don't steal, work hard, so that you will have resources to give to the poor;

- If you have something to say, let it be something that helps, and not a word that is destructive; at times you will be angry, but do not become obsessive in your anger; through it Satan will destroy you;

- Forgive because, after all, Christ has forgiven you.

A new life—there is a wrecking ball, positioned just outside the house. Whether we are fifteen or thirty-five or fifty-five or seventy-five, it is a word for us: We are called to *conversion*. Not only at one time along the journey but at every step, God has this word for us: I have saved you by my grace; I am calling you to a new life.

This has been a learning for me about the ministry. In the last book before his death, Henri Nouwen wrote these words about the new life through the imagery of travel into a new country:

You have an idea of what the new country looks like. Still, you are very much at home, although not truly at peace, in the old country. You know the ways of the old country, its joys and pains, its happy and sad moments. You have spent most of your days there. Even though you know that you have not found there what your heart most desires, you remain quite attached to it. It has become part of your very bones.

Now you have come to realize that you must leave it and enter the new country where your Beloved dwells. You know that what helped and guided you in the old country no longer works, but what else do you have to go by? You are being asked to trust that you will find what you need in the new country. That requires the death of what has become so precious to you: influence, success, yes, even affection and praise.

Trust is so hard, since you have nothing to fall back on. Still, trust is what is essential. The new country is where you are called to go, and the only way to go there is naked and vulnerable. It seems that you keep crossing and recrossing the border. For a while you experience a real joy in the new country. But then you feel afraid and start longing again for all you left behind, so you go back to the old country. To your dismay, you discover the old country has lost its charm. Risk a few more steps into the new country, trusting that each time your enter it, you will feel more comfortable and be able to stay longer.[17]

The word that speaks to me in this meditation is *trust*. We do not trust God at only one point in our lives. We trust God at every point along the way. And the new country for us might be going into middle school or high school or college, or getting married, or living in a new place or finding work, or having a child, or the death of a parent, or retirement or our own illness.

In the ministry I am always calling people to trust. And, of course, I am always asking myself, *Ken, how much do you really trust God?* Read the fourth chapter of

Ephesians again. In the first third you will sense a new pattern for the mission of Jesus: It belongs to us. In the middle third of the chapter, you will see God's vision for the church: that it matures, growing up into Jesus who is the head. And in the last third, you will be challenged to leave the old life behind and to trust God for a new life.

How has my mind changed about the ministry?

The mission belongs to us.
God is calling us to grow up.
And the invitation is to trust the Lord.

So be it, in the name of the Father, the Son, and the Holy Spirit. Amen.

CHAPTER EIGHT

A Consumer's Guide to Spiritual Gift Resources and Inventories

Like good stewards of the manifold grace of God, serve one another with whatever gift each of you has received.

(1 Peter 4:10)

The following is a brief description of several resources in the area of spiritual gifts. Call it a Consumer's Guide.

Body Building: Creating a Ministry Team Through Spiritual Gifts
by Brian Bauknight
(Nashville: Abingdon Press, 1996, 112 pages)

Focus: The author helps the reader to understand spiritual gifts within the context of building a multiple staff. The author draws from his own personal experiences and writes in a style that is accessible and engaging. The book also includes a good balance between narrative experience and leadership theory.
Audience: This work would be an excellent resource for ministry teams in local churches, especially large and/or growing congregations. The appendix would also be helpful to staff-parish relations committees.
Strengths: The book has an extremely practical focus. Bauknight discusses staff meetings, calling staff members who are church members, position descriptions, and relationships between senior and associate pastors.

Weaknesses: The only weaknesses lie in the temptation of the reader to see this book as a roadmap for his or her congregation. Instead, I hope the reader will be inspired to work with the same issues, and with a similar intentionality, in his or her own setting.

Spirit Gifts: One Spirit, Many Gifts
by Patricia Brown
(Nashville: Abingdon Press, 1996, 89 pages)

Focus: This is a brief work that will help individuals in a workshop setting to learn more about their spiritual gifts. It speaks to a number of issues surrounding spiritual gifts and includes an inventory (52 questions) and a variety of exercises that will help the participant to define his or her gifts.

Audience: The Participant's Workbook could be used by members of congregations and is written at a very basic level. Individuals with little or no biblical background would be comfortable with this resource.

Strengths: The workbook is clear and easy to understand. It connects biblical references to spiritual gifts with contemporary experiences (for example, the gift of prophecy is linked with the ministry of Martin Luther King, Jr.). Brown brings the sometimes complicated language of the gifts of the Holy Spirit to an appropriate level for seekers.

Weaknesses: Because of the work's brevity, some important dimensions of gifts are neglected, such as the controversies surrounding some of the gifts and the difficulties in fitting the gifts together into the Body of Christ. This resource may not be the best available for leaders in congregations who have a broader background in Scripture and other studies of the faith.

Network: The Right People, in the Right Places, for the Right Reasons
by Bruce Bugbeem, Don Cousins, and Bill Hybels
(Grand Rapids: Zondervan, 1994, 149 pages)

Focus: The authors see a core value of the church as placing individuals in ministry that flows from their passions, spiritual gifts, and personal styles. The resource includes an inventory (133 questions) and a feedback questionnaire to be completed by three outside persons who know the participant.

Audience: This is a thorough instrument, designed for congregations that have a high level of commitment to ministry. It is most appropriate to corporate cultures where feedback is a normal part of daily life. Finally, its complexity is best suited to large membership churches that have the infrastructure to utilize it.

Strengths: The summary of spiritual gifts in section 5 is excellent, and the connection to servanthood in section 6 is also helpful. The "passion assessment" (section 2) also helps the participant to relate gift to a specific call.

Weaknesses: Individuals will need a high degree of motivation to complete this process. It comes out of the life of Willow Creek Community Church in Chicago, and may or may not be transferrable to other settings.

Rediscovering the Charismata
by Charles Bryant
(Waco: Word, 1986, 172 pages)

Focus: The book's subtitle is "Building Up the Body of Christ Through Spiritual Gifts." The author clearly has the local church in focus in this discussion of gifts, and parish realities are always kept clearly before the reader.

Audience: This book contains more detailed descriptions of the spiritual gifts than many other resources, and would be helpful to a pastor preparing to lead a Bible study or to a Sunday school teacher in his or her own preparation. The book will also be of interest to those who want to know more about spiritual gifts in general.

Strengths: The author gives a careful analysis of each of the spiritual gifts, including meanings of the Greek terms. There is also a helpful process for understanding and utilizing gifts within the local church.

Weaknesses: The author, following the practice of many other authors, draws too neat a distinction between gifts and fruit of the Spirit, and between gifts and offices.

Discerning Your Spiritual Gifts
by Lloyd Edwards
(Cambridge: Cowley, 1988, 144 pages)

Focus: The author writes from within the Anglican tradition, and yet the resource could be adapted to a variety of settings. There is a gifts inventory (25 questions) and a model that could be used for a weekend retreat or on a number of evenings.

Audience: This book is written for pastors, leaders, and members of congregations. At one level it is simple, and yet there is great wisdom in this resource. Serious individuals who want to relate the gifts to their life experiences will find this work invaluable.

Strengths: The chapter on Christian tradition goes beyond that offered in other books, and the discussion of the relationship between wounds and gifts adds depth to the understanding of healing ministry.

Weaknesses: Leaders in congregations will need to develop their own specific plans in utilizing this resource, which is not as detailed in its outline.

Eighth Day of Creation
by Elizabeth O'Connor
(Waco: Word, 1971, 115 pages)

Focus: This book grew out of the life and mission of the Church of the Saviour in Washington, D.C. O'Connor explores the relationship between gifts and creativity, and she weaves together the story of her own experience with spiritual exercises and devotional readings.

Audience: This work is a classic that has influenced a number of the later works in spiritual gifts. It will be helpful for those who lead retreats in the area of spiritual gifts and for those who want to engage in a contemplative or centering prayer exercise related to gifts.

Strengths: This is a work of tremendous spiritual depth. After three decades it remains timeless. It also speaks to the important link between creativity and gifts, which oddly enough, is absent in most works in the field of spiritual gifts.

Weaknesses: This work will require some translation on the part of the leader and is best suited to those who lean toward the contemplative stream of the Christian tradition.

The Purpose Driven Church
by Rick Warren
(Grand Rapids: Zondervan, 1995, 399 pages)

Focus: This is a work that draws from the experience of the Saddleback Valley Community Church in Southern California and is written by its pastor, Rick Warren. This large-membership church has a very specific mission and purpose built around "Life Development Process." A part of that process is S.H.A.P.E.: "Spiritual gifts, heart, abilities, personality, experiences."

Audience: This work will benefit pastors and leaders of

congregations who want to become more focused in their corporate missions and in their work with individuals and their gifts. A variety of types of churches could find this to be a useful resource.

Strengths: This is a very "user-friendly" process that could be adapted to different contexts. The discussion of gifts is balanced and at a medium level of complexity. The author also gives a helpful critique of spiritual gift inventories.

Weaknesses: The process will be only as effective as those who are implementing it.

Devotional Classics,
edited by Richard Foster and James Bryan Smith
(San Francisco: Harper San Francisco, 1993, 272 pages)
A Spiritual Formation Workbook, by James Bryan Smith
(San Francisco: Harper San Francisco, 1993, 96 pages)
Streams of Living Water, by Richard Foster
(San Francisco: Harper San Francisco, 1998, 256 pages)

Focus: These works develop an integrated theory about six traditions of spiritual practice among Christians: contemplative, holiness, charismatic, social justice, evangelical, and incarnational. The *Devotional Classics* includes readings from spiritual authors in each tradition. The *Workbook* is a group process for encountering each of the traditions and responding to them in prayer, study, and action. *Streams of Living Water* is a history of Christian spirituality. Although not about spiritual gifts, these resources parallel the diversity of gifts within the Body of Christ.

Audience: Pastors and laity who want to grow more deeply in the Christian life and who are willing to appreciate differences among Christians.

Strengths: A very comprehensive system of thought.
Weaknesses: This is a confessional Christian approach

that is also ecumenical in breadth. The weaknesses are difficult to locate!

Your Spiritual Gifts Can Help Your Church Grow
by Peter Wagner
(Ventura, California: Regal, 1979, 272 pages)

Focus: Peter Wagner is an authority on church growth who has taught at Fuller Theological Seminary. The author is convinced that spiritual gifts are crucial to the growth of the world-wide Christian mission. This work includes a spiritual inventory that contains 125 questions.

Audience: This book is well suited for evangelical churches and for pastors who serve in missionary contexts. It can also be read with profit by pastors and leaders of mainline churches.

Strengths: Wagner is well versed in the literature of spiritual gifts, and he is especially helpful in linking them to issues like martyrdom, deliverance, and intercession in ways not often found in other books. He also has a realistic appraisal of the promise and peril of spiritual gifts.

Weaknesses: Wagner can sometimes focus on the extraordinary and the exceptional to the exclusion of the ways in which gifts are employed in congregations.

Discovering Your Gifts, Vision and Call
by Jacqueline McMakin and Rhoda Nary
(San Francisco: Harper San Francisco, 1993, 113 pages)

Focus: The authors, who have been influenced by the Church of the Saviour and the Shalem Institute, develop an understanding of spiritual gifts in relation to God's vision for the world and our calling in response to that vision.

Audience: This resource will be helpful to individuals

seeking to make a difference in their communities and for congregations who are ready to employ their gifts in the larger society.

Strengths: The design of this resource is practical and easily implemented. The authors also develop the prophetic gifts in helpful ways.

Weaknesses: The book's strength is also its weakness. Many of the spiritual gifts are not articulated or evoked in this book, and so it may be more applicable to some participants than to others.

Spiritual Gifts on the World Wide Web

The following congregations and ministries have made intentional attempts to minister out of a framework of spiritual gifts. Again, they are representative, and you will want to consider the gifts of your own congregations as you learn from them!

www.umcservant.org Church of the Servant, Oklahoma City, Oklahoma

www. willowcreek.org Willow Creek Community Church, South Barrington, Illinois

www.saddleback.com , Saddleback Valley Community Church, Mission Viejo, California

www.stephenministries.org Stephen Ministries, St. Louis, Missouri

www.upperroom.org, Upper Room, Nashville, Tennessee

CHAPTER NINE

The Journey Toward
Our Spiritual Gifts

*By grace you have been saved through faith, and
this is not your own doing; it is the gift of God—
not the result of works, so that no one may boast.
For we are what he has made us, created in Christ
Jesus for good works, which God prepared before-
hand to be our way of life.*

(*Ephesians 2:8-10*)

*We live the given life,
And not the planned.*
(*Wendell Berry,* Sabbath Poems)

The mainline churches are aware of a deep spiritual
hunger in our culture. Eugene Peterson may be correct in
noting that this hunger may be a sign that all is not well;
nevertheless, it seems to be present. And its presence
leads to questions:

- Where does a pastor find help when the well
  runs dry?
- How can local congregations respond to this
  hunger?
- Where do annual conferences go to find
  resources for renewal?

These questions have been woven into my experiences
as a United Methodist pastor serving in a variety of roles
within the church. Several years ago I was asked to get
involved with our annual conference in the area of

spiritual formation. I was sent to a consultation at the Upper Room led by Janice Grana, Steve Bryant, David Watson, Danny Morris, and others. One of the recurring themes out of that event was the conviction that congregations could go no further spiritually than their pastors. A task force on spiritual formation was formed, with the hope of creating a climate where pastors could focus on their own spiritual journeys and claim their spiritual gifts, as diverse as they are. A couple of years later I was given the opportunity to help form a new congregation, work that was very demanding, stimulating, rewarding, chaotic, and draining. The spiritual life of the pastor, I quickly discovered, is essential to the growth and health of a new church.[1]

The Importance of Working on Our Own Spiritual Lives

I return to my foundational questions: How do we find spiritual renewal, regardless of our role or context? In the midst of these responsibilities I heard a lecture on the art and poetry of Thomas Merton, given by Michael Mott, who has written what is almost universally considered to be the definitive biography of Merton.[2] One statement he made caught my attention: *"Merton was never interested in giving other people spiritual advice. He simply wanted to work on his own spiritual life."* When I later shared this statement with Ed Friedman, the family systems theorist who developed the concept of self-differentiation for clergy, he simply smiled and said, *"Bingo!"*

There was for me a connection (an appropriate word for United Methodists), and I became convinced that others would be the beneficiaries if pastors, like Merton, engaged in the task of personal spiritual renewal.

This realization led me to a renewed engagement with the life and works of Thomas Merton, the Trappist monk, peace activist, celebrity, artist, poet, and best-selling author. What follows is an attempt to draw together his own reflections on the spiritual journey, especially as it relates to the call of God and the gifts that we are given.

I am convinced that the crisis in the pastoral ministry is a spiritual crisis. In *The Wisdom of the Desert*, Merton reflects on the movement of the monks into the desert to pray. He writes:

> To leave the world, is, in fact, to help save it in saving oneself. . . . The Coptic hermits who left the world as though escaping from a wreck did not merely intend to save themselves. They knew that they were helpless to do any good for others as long as they floundered around in the wreckage. But once they got a foothold on solid ground, things were different. Then they had not only the power but the obligation to pull the whole world to safety after them.[3]

The most important reality in our congregational life is the relationship between a pastor and God. If this relationship is attended to and nurtured, other relationships have the potential to be strong and healthy. I am not being escapist. I am simply noting the dangers that are present within and outside our congregations, and indeed the dangers within us. If we flounder, our churches either self-destruct or spend their energies parenting us. Either outcome is dysfunctional.

Reading Merton has helped me to reflect on a variety of issues: my relationship to God, my relationship to the congregation, the relationship between parents and children. One of the best things we can do for ourselves as pastors is to work on our own spiritual lives. *And an essential dimension of that work is to identify our own spiritual gifts!* (See chapter 5.) Practically, this means continuing to be present to God in a variety of ways, such as days apart, spiritual direction, silent retreat, tools for self-awareness, Bible study, accountability, and support in groups. But the availability of these experiences leads to two questions:

- How can these experiences become the norm for pastors?
- And how can attending to our spiritual lives become a matter of course for our life "in conference"?

The Meaning of Journey

At the Upper Room I heard a presentation by Bruce Ough, at that time a member of the Iowa Conference and now Resident Bishop West Ohio Conference, The United Methodist Church. He described four criteria for pastoral appointment-making in the annual conference in which he served:

- Does this person have skills in proclamation?
- Does this person have relational skills?
- Does this person have administrative skills?
- Is this person on a spiritual journey?

In reading Merton one comes to know a person who is on a spiritual journey. This was evident in the evolution of his thought, in his relationships with his peers and his superiors, in the depth of his writing, and in his orientation to the world. For Merton, life itself was a pilgrimage, a journey. This is perhaps best expressed in the well-known prayer found in *Thoughts in Solitude:*

> My Lord God, I have no idea where I am going. I do not see the road ahead of me. I cannot know for certain where it will end. . . . I will not fear, for you are ever with me, and you will never leave me to face my perils alone.[4]

This statement surely has much to say about the experience of itineracy: the unknown outcomes, the necessity of faith, the willingness to risk, the knowledge that God is always with us, echoing Psalm 23. Surely we have experienced the emotions present in the above prayer as we have entered new appointments; surely we have questioned our own motives; surely we have looked back and known that God has walked beside us. Ministry, as in other areas of life, is an unfolding journey: We are unsure about the future, but we know that the Lord will be with us.

Stability and Itineracy

Merton's sense of pilgrimage coexisted uneasily with his sense of place, in the vow of stability. He once wrote: *"As soon as God gets you in one monastery you want to be in another one."* A good deal of the early part of *The Sign of Jonas* deals with a fundamental struggle: Should Merton be a Cistercian or a Carthusian? Gradually this question becomes unimportant, as Merton works on other, more important issues.

Stability has to do with making peace with where we are and focusing on the gifts of God that are placed in that community. The temptation, and Merton would have called it a temptation, is to see the next place as a spiritual utopia: It never is. The spiritual life happens where we are, in the present. Merton once wrote the following about prayer:

> In prayer we discover what we already have. You start where you are and you deepen what you already have, and you realize that you are already there. We already have everything, but we don't know it, and we don't experience it. Everything has been given to us in Christ. All we need to do is experience what we already possess.[5]

Do we miss the real meaning of ministry in the places where we are serving because we are always looking to move to another place? What if there is no "greener pasture" anywhere else, only the same issues (self and others) to be dealt with in a new environment? What can we learn from the monastic vow of stability within a polity of itineracy? Merton's words about being at Gethsemani might be helpful ones for us to ponder in our settings: God *"has put me in this place because He wants me in this place, and if He ever wants to put me anywhere else, He will do so in a way that will leave no doubt as to who is doing it."*[6]

Being Ourselves: What Is False and What Is True

In *Merton's Palace of Nowhere*, James Finley describes Merton's thought in light of a key image: the concept of the false and true self. The false self is denial of who we are, the rejection of our identity and thus the rejection of God. The expression of the false self leads to lies and illusions. The true self, on the other hand, is our whole self before God, the self in communion with God. We are called to the "forward journey back to our original identity in God."[7]

For Wesleyans, this is the process of sanctification, the renewal of the image of God in us. The long shadow of the false self leads us to pretense, hiding, concealment, blaming—all characteristic of Adam (Genesis 3). The true self is embraced as we live in communion with God in the world and is discovered through the disciplines of solitude and silence.[8]

How does this relate to ministry? Our connection, our churches, have been deeply affected by experiences over the past few years, experiences of hiding, concealment, blaming, falsehood, and deception. These experiences have been with us since the beginning of time, to be sure, but in our present context they are more likely to become public. There is, in the society, a greater demand for integrity among public servants, and this includes pastors who have representative ministries. The implications of the "false self," often among the most gifted, live themselves out in our relationships with each other; and as pastors have access to the intimate lives of others, the potential danger is obvious. This leads to the necessity for spiritual renewal, accountability, and evaluation. I am convinced that Merton would have been quite comfortable with such practices and systems; indeed, he would have been the first to note our capacity to deceive ourselves. And yet we have been given a great deal of freedom, as human beings and as pastors, a freedom Merton interprets in the following way:

> God leaves us free to be whatever we like. We can be ourselves, or not, as we please. We are at liberty to be real, or to be unreal. We may be true or false, the choice is ours. We may wear now one mask and now another, and never, if we so desire, appear with our own true face.
>
> To work out our identity in God, which the Bible calls "working out our salvation," is a labor that requires sacrifice and anguish, risk and many tears.[9]

We are called to work out our identity in God, to work out our own salvation, to come to the discovery of our own gifts for ministry. And yet the interior calling is always lived out in community. Have we, as United Methodists and North American Christians, valued freedom more than community? Merton valued community, even as he saw that community for what it was:

> I am part of Gethsemani. I belong to the family. It is a family about which I have no illusions. And the most satisfying thing about this sense of incorporation is

that I am glad to belong to this community, not another, and to be bred flesh and bone into the same body as these brothers and not other ones. Their imperfections and my own remain as obvious as ever, but they no longer seem to make any difference.[10]

When Merton recognized the truth about himself, he seemed to be able to see his community and to participate in that community without illusions. That, it seems to me, is the process by which people are empowered to take off their masks.

Neill Hamilton, in *Maturing in the Christian Life*, describes the fundamental transition in the pastoral ministry as movement from the "discipleship phase" to "life in the spirit." The discipleship phase mirrors the illusion of the disciples that Jesus would reestablish the golden age of the Davidic kingdom. "This misperception of the kingdom of God and of Jesus' role in it," Hamilton suggests, "is the grand illusion of discipleship." Hamilton's description of the implications of this illusion for pastors is striking:

> Most of us respond to a call to ministry with particular, beloved and effective clergypersons in mind. As we observe their ministry we see God challenging human lives with the transforming power of the gospel. Since we long for such challenge and transformation, we suppose the people in those congregations do also . . . prospective ministers are able to sustain their dream of ministry until their first call or appointment to parish leadership after graduation from seminary and full ordination. Then the reality of the profession tumbles in on them. The reality is that the vast majority of persons in a typical congregation do not want themselves or their world to be transformed by the gospel.[11]

Like the disciples, we can overcome our illusions only as we honestly face them through our own emptiness.

Paradoxically, at this moment, we are open to the indwelling spirit. As Hamilton summarizes it, we trade the "eschatology of career" (or I would add, institutional survival) for "readiness for ministry in the Spirit." Again, Merton can be a wonderful example, having given up prestige and opportunity in order to attain silence and, ultimately, God.

Gifts and Vocation

Merton was engaged in a lifelong struggle with his own identity. His particular question was, Can I be a writer and a monk? Merton had a strong desire for solitude, and yet he had a gift for writing, a gift that would make solitude difficult if not impossible. In entering the monastery Merton had considered writing to be in his past; then, by God's providence perhaps, he was given a superior who commanded that he do just that—write. For this reason Merton would comment in the following way: *"An author in a Trappist monastery is like a duck in a chicken coop."*[12]

This question is often posed, verbally or nonverbally, by pastors: Do I fit here? Can I be myself and be a part of the system? Do I have to give up a core part of myself in order to serve the church and God?

The answers to those questions, for Merton and for us, have a way of working themselves out. Merton made peace with the call to write, indeed flourished in that vocation. Many of us find that if we are open to a process of discernment, God will also use our gifts, the essence of who we are, in our service to the church and the world. Indeed, this is our primary calling as pastors!

God

"Do you suppose I have a spiritual life? I have none . . . for I have renounced spirituality to find God."[13]

Appropriating the work of Thomas Merton for mainline pastors at the beginning of the twenty-first century is a risky endeavor. Spiritual formation is a "hot topic" and an interest of almost any institutional grouping that has its ear to the ground. To get in on this trend, we may assume that we simply take Merton and his life and thought and impose him onto our structures, systems, and agendas.

Yielding to this temptation would be neither helpful to us nor true to Merton. Merton was most insightful in pointing us toward those areas of life that were most susceptible to self-deception. He was keenly aware that schedules, agendas, and structures often got in the way of a relationship with God.

In Merton we see a human being who lived in the midst of an elaborate system, one designed to nourish the spiritual life. His participation in that system, and his critique of it, can help us as we seek to know, love, and bear witness to God as pastors. Merton had no illusions about himself or his tradition. As a young monk Merton wrote "Gethsemani is the spring where I am to drink of the waters of life, and if I look elsewhere, it is to a broken cistern." Other spiritual options have led our culture at times to broken cisterns; there are rich resources from within our own traditions, and indeed within our own congregations. A Trappist monastery was, for Merton, a conducive setting to engage in the life of the spirit, even with its imperfections. And a local congregation is an appropriate context to work on our own spiritual lives. Merton did not intend to renew the church or to inspire those outside the walls of Gethsemani. He simply worked on his own spiritual life. And as we engage in that task, God will bring renewal to the Body of Christ, the church, and to the world.

My Relationship with God

When I focus on my relationship with God,
I am on the way to spiritual health.
When I am preoccupied with the failures of others,
I am on the way to spiritual illness.

Jesus asks, *"Do you want to be healed?"*

When I am connected to others,
I am on the way to wholeness.
When I am isolated from others,
I am disoriented and in spiritual danger.

Jesus says, *"I am the vine, you are the branches."*

I am at my best when my thoughts, my actions,
my emotions have a singular focus:
the Lord's will, desire, dream for me.
All other things are then given their places of
importance, priority, proportion.

If I focus on the failures of others,
I am probably avoiding a matter of greater importance:
my relationship with God.

Jesus says, *"Seek first God's kingdom and righteousness."*

If I isolate myself from others,
wholeness proceeds to disintegration,
strength becomes weakness,
hope becomes despair.
Jesus says, *"Where two or three are gathered in my name,
I am in their midst."*

To the extent that I can accept myself as a child of God,
I can know a life of blessing. I can be saved.

Jesus says, *"Peace I leave with you, my peace I give to you."*

There is no more important task
than to tend to my own spiritual life.
The "God" question is more important
than any other.

Why do I avoid it?
Why do I neglect it?
Why do I postpone it?

Jesus says, *"I am the way, and the truth, and the life."*

—K. H. C.

CHAPTER TEN

A Sending Forth:
Spiritual Gifts Without
Easy Answers

*Let us not grow weary in doing what is right, for
we will reap at harvest time, if we do not give up.*
(Galatians 6:9)

*The one who began a good work among you will
bring it to completion by the day of Jesus Christ.*
(Philippians 1:6)

*The overall health and functioning of any organi-
zation depend primarily on one or two people at
the top, and that is true whether the relationship
system is a personal family, a sports team, an
orchestra, a congregation, a religious hierarchy, or
an entire nation.*
(Edwin Friedman, Generation to Generation*)*

Spiritual gifts are a part of our heritage, our birthright
as pastors of mainline congregations. And yet we have
ignored them, marginalizing them to a corner of
American evangelicalism, fundamentalism, or pente-
costalism. That we have done so is in part due to our
training—the gifts of the spirit are not as prevalent as,
say, justification by faith in our understanding of Paul's
theology, due to the Reformation's influence upon us.[1]
Many of us may have had unpleasant, unpredictable, or
even unexplainable experiences with folk who are
"filled" with the spirit.

And yet, God gives these gifts to the Body, the church.

If we do not avoid them, neither can we easily or neatly categorize them. They defy simple definition. The gifts emerge, erupt, sometimes blessing, sometime cursing. They are a mystery. Gifts are instruments of power and vessels of grace.

They are a part of our tradition, and we cannot ignore them in the work of the ministry. And so, a simple strategy, a sending forth. The following suggestions are borrowed from a wonderful book by Ronald Heifetz on leadership. These seven suggestions, adapted from his advice to leaders, will help pastors in understanding and employing spiritual gifts.

Getting on the Balcony

As pastors we are participants in the lives of congregations, but we are also observers. It helps, at times, "to get far enough above the fray to see the key patterns," according to Heifetz. For the pastor, those patterns are embedded in Scripture and in tradition. Are two key members in conflict with one another? When we gain a balcony perspective, we recall the letter to Philippians, Paul's word of admonition, *"I urge Euodia and I urge Syntyche to be of the same mind in the Lord"* (4:2); and with some detachment we are able to see the pattern. Is there a turf battle going on between differing areas of the church? From our place in the balcony we can see the subtle movements around the key players and perhaps begin to identify the key issues.

We can almost hear Paul, again, speaking to the Corinthians, *"It has been reported to me by some of Chloe's people that there are quarrels among you, my brothers and sisters. What I mean is that each of you says, 'I belong to Paul,' or 'I belong to Apollos,' or 'I belong to Cephas,' or 'I belong to Christ'"* (1 Corinthians 1:11-12).

A knowledge of Scripture can help us to see in fresh

ways the mission of the church and the conflicts that arise. A knowledge of church history can help us to see the ways in which we are repeating past errors, committing former sins, but also reclaiming lost treasures. A knowledge of the culture can help us to see the ways in which we are shaped, even subconsciously, by the world which can be at odds with the gospel.

For this reason I am skeptical about the trend, celebrated in some church growth circles, that large congregations will assume the role of theological education in the future. The positive contribution of the large church is that it is immersed in the drama of God's mission, in ways that are impossible for theological schools. The strength of the seminary or divinity school, however, is that it teaches this balcony perspective. And pastors who do the difficult work of ministry will find it essential to escape to the balcony from time to time.

It occurs to me that the balcony might be a wonderful image for the resurrection life into which we are invited.

For Reflection: Is there a situation in your congregation that might benefit from your spending some time in the balcony?

For Meditation:

Arise

A vision of the future leads me forward,
but to see it I must die to self,
like a grain of wheat
buried in the earth.

Jesus the guide tells me to "let go"
of everything that is not God,
and to follow his path,
a path of righteousness and peace.

What keeps me from walking with God?
My need to be in control,
my desire to find my own direction,
my hesitancy to loosen my grip,

and to free fall
into the hands of the One
who created me, and loves me,
and prepares a future for me.

And after a time of death
there is surely a time to arise,
to come before the Lord with singing,
to cry out with joy to the God of my salvation.
—K. H. C.

The Role/Self Distinction

Leaders, Heifetz argues, see a distinction between themselves and their roles. In other words, we are more than our functions. We value being rather than simply doing. Here pastors need the biblical command and gift of the sabbath, against the cultural pressure toward workaholism. When our work becomes our lives, boundaries are blurred. These boundaries might be self and role, or pastor and church, or church and family, or church and God, or self and God. A good friend once commented to me that perhaps it is not as helpful for pastors to model themselves after Jesus as it is for the church to model itself after the Body of Christ! Underneath that sentence was a warning against our tendency to become messiah figures when all is going well, or martyrs when all is not.

A healthy distinction between role and self helps us to get a life! It helps us to have breathing space in our lives for family, friendship, fun. When we are able to distinguish between ourselves and our roles, we are reminded that God loves us not only for what we do but for who we are! And only then can we serve out of that self-understanding with others. Any honest pastor will admit that, while we want to serve out of motivations of grace and unconditional love, we can easily value members of our congregations not for who they are, but for what they do, in other words, for their productivity. We might even condemn a corporate culture that uses people even as we are tempted in the same direction. *We believe—God, help our unbelief!*

Pastors will benefit from this simple distinction. A diagnosis here is apparent when pastors retire from active ministry. Some enjoy a slower pace, pursue hobbies, discover ways to serve the Kingdom. Others are lost; they have *fused* themselves with their roles, and with the loss of role comes the loss of self. I say this not as judgment but as observation.

I speak out of some personal experience with the blurring of this distinction. For some years I served in a ministry role in which I was, at the time, almost perfectly suited. The church was growing, and my areas of ministry—discipleship, missions, evangelism—were prospering. This was due in part to timing, in part to groundwork laid by my predecessors, in part due to gifted lay leaders. In a period of a few short years the Disciple Bible Study was begun, the Stephen Ministry with more than forty active laity was initiated, a semi-annual mission to Bolivia was established, a relationship with a nearby Divinity School where professors came to teach biblical studies was flourishing, a confirmation mentoring program was developed.

And on and on. It was exhilarating. And I was not approaching burnout. I had become completely immersed in the work. There was, however, a down side. My self was fused with my work. I could not clearly see the difference between who I was as a person, or even as a child of God, and who I was as a minister of that congregation. There was no critical distance. There were no boundaries in my life. The role/self distinction had become blurred.

How can we maintain the distinction? We can gain a larger perspective on life through relationships with persons who are outside our congregations. We can listen to the wisdom of those who are farther along life's journey. We can detach through an occasional day apart. We may seek the counsel of a spiritual director. We can open ourselves to the larger gifts that God has placed in our lives. Sometimes these are family or friendship. Sometimes they are shaped by geography or the arts or a sport or a passion. Our roles will take on a greater strength if we can distinguish them from some other area of our lives that also gives us contentment, joy, and peace. Sometimes we need a rest from our roles. And sometimes gifted people need that rest the most!

For Reflection: How do you share your spiritual gifts in ways that have nothing to do with your work as a pastor?

For Meditation:

Rest

Thou hast made us for thyself, O Lord,
and our hearts are restless until they find their rest
in Thee.
(Saint Augustine, Fourth Century)

You call us to walk with you,
and yet you invite us into your rest.
We become involved in the journey;
and before we are aware, we have lost our way.

We are walking, but to which destination?
The maps are lost, the guides are unsure.

We want to follow, but we aren't sure
how to cross over, how to discover again
the way that leads to life.

There is a restlessness within us,
an addiction to the pace;
and the voice, which we can hear
in its faintness, says to us,
"My yoke is easy, my burden is light."

Walk with us again, Lord, in the journey
that fulfils our purpose for being here;
ease our restless hearts,
welcome us into your rest.

—K. H. C.

Externalizing the Conflict

It is easy to personalize conflict, to internalize stress. In reading the Scriptures, I am amazed at Paul's ability to respond to the chaos of the church of Corinth through the framework of gifts. He does not avoid the conflict. He does not blame. And he does not personalize the issue. In Heifetz's language, he eternalizes the conflict.

This is easier said than done. The difficulty lies in our egocentrism. Consider: When a member of your congregation comes to you and says, "I need to meet with you soon; I have a problem to talk with you about." What is your first thought? If you are honest, you probably begin to think, *Oh, no, there is some church crisis that I don't know about. . . . There is some fire that I am going to need to respond to.*

In the great majority of instances when this has happened and the member comes later, the issue is about something else: a parent-child disagreement; a marital issue; an addiction; a need for reconciliation with a friend or coworker. My egocentrism leads me to personalize the conflict.

This is critical for pastors to grasp, because churches are filled with conflict. The twenty-first century North American church is filled with conflict, as were the first-century churches of Galatia, Philippi, and Corinth.

For Reflection: Is there an issue in your congregational setting that has become too personal for you?

For Meditation:

Criticism

When others are critical, you take it personally.
It hits hard, at the core of your being;
and with even a brief comment
the seed of caustic judgment or corrective advice
is planted within you.
In time that seed grows into a harvest of self-doubt,
and you question your direction, your self.
The criticism blankets and covers you,
and you become paralyzed.

It will help you to remember
that Jesus holds you in his grace.
Yes, it will also help you to locate
the kernel of truth
that is found in the critical word.
Learn from it,
but do not dwell on it.
Being a human being, you are imperfect.

The critical word will help you most
in understanding the person who speaks it.
When others are critical of you,
do not take it personally.

Live in God's grace, the Lord's peace,
the Spirit's comfort.
Only in this way
will you make spiritual progress.
The paralysis will lift,
and you will enter into a new day.
—K. H. C.

Partners

"Leadership cannot be exercised alone," Heifetz writes.
"The lone-warrior model of leadership is heroic suicide." We
are all tempted by the *great man* or *great woman* theory of
leadership, even as it is applied to ministry. The
brochures come to us, with blurbs about a person's ministry in which attendance has quadrupled, membership
has tripled, financial giving has doubled. We glance
again at the pastor; we think about the results. A mixture
of envy, jealousy, and admiration arises in us. *What a great
man or woman,* we say to ourselves.

Most current theories of leadership give emphasis to
the greatness of teams, of alliances, of partnerships. We
do not exercise our spiritual gifts alone. The gift of
preaching is strengthened by music, the pastoral ministry shared during the week, and the administrative
details that are covered in preparation for Sunday worship. All work together to give the sermon a context of
mission within a setting of inspiration in the midst of a
community that rejoices and suffers together.

Heifetz speaks of two types of partners: *confidants* and
allies. Confidants are coworkers, often with other gifts,
who help us to see things in perspective. In my own
experience I have worked on multiple staffs that were
true partnerships. I understand this is not always the
case, and when it occurs it is a gift of God's grace. But
when a musician, an educator, and a pastor, or two
or three pastors can appreciate each others' gift and

171

contribution to the whole of the Body, a synergy does emerge. The opposite is also true: When facets of church ministry become divided along the areas of staff responsibility, much energy is drained away from the mission of Christ and into a church structure that maintains a conflictual equilibrium.

Confidants are also friends. Those who do the work of ministry are nourished by the presence of friendships. A missing link in the discussions of vocation and calling, and their relationship with self-fulfillment, has been identified by the ethicist Gilbert Meilaender as friendship.[3] It may be that vocation was never meant to carry the full freight of meaning and purpose in life; perhaps friendship was intended to serve that purpose. Confidants help us to see the work of ministry in proper perspective.

Allies, in Heifetz's language, most closely parallel the role of the mentor in spiritual gifts (see chapter 4). For the reader, this can be understood in a couple of ways. First, we can recall those who have identified and cultivated our spiritual gifts. And second, we can look within our own Christian experiences to those whose gifts need our encouragement. Mentors make the expression of our gifts possible. And in our own positions of authority, we can be the patrons of the gifts of others.

For Reflection: Can you identify, and give thanks for someone who has been a partner with you in God's mission? Someone who has been a patron of your spiritual gifts? Someone who might benefit from your own encouragement?

Self-Examination

Leaders must know enough about themselves to perceive their own biases in order to compensate for them, Heifetz insists. Pastors have genuine difficulty receiving helpful and honest feedback. The laity are not always sure that the pastor really wants criticism. Others may not feel that they are in a position to give feedback. Pastors may undertake continuing education that gives feedback about preaching or leadership style, but there remains a need for self-examination.

There is, in our Christian tradition, a rich heritage of self-examination. It reaches back to the Psalms (Psalm 51, for example) and continues through disciplines such as the *examen of consciousness.*[4] Our motives are not always pure, our vision not always clear, our desires not always healthy. Because we are sinners, we are in need of disciplines that filter out skewed perspectives.

Craig Dykstra, in *Vision and Character,* reflects on the importance of the transformed imagination, and the disciplines—repentance, prayer, service—that sustain such a practice. *Repentance* is a necessary complement to our practice of spiritual gifts: sometimes we neglect our gifts, we project them onto others, we exalt them above those of others. *Prayer* is attention to God, and to the image of God in ourselves. For what purpose has God created us? Do we sometimes attempt to be something other than ourselves? Prayer as attention also involves receiving the gifts of God from others. *Service,* according to Dykstra, *"is a discipline of renouncing power in order to be present with others in vulnerability, equality and compassion. . . . It repeatedly has the effect of providing space for other persons to tap their own resources and to gather their own energies."*[5] These disciplines—repentance, prayer, service—Dykstra argues, shape the moral life. I would also argue that they shape the practice of our spiritual gifts.

- Without repentance, we are prone to arrogance.

- Without prayer, our gifts, our ministries, our institutions become idols.

- Without service, our gifts are lost in the language of office and position, status and role; and we abuse the power that belongs to the One who came not to be served, but to serve (Mark 10:45).

Our disciplines of repentance, prayer, and service are essential in our continued self-examination.

For Reflection: Can you spend a moment in self-examination? How have you neglected a gift? How have your gifts been used to glorify God?

For Meditation:

A Spiritual Audit

1. Have my most significant religious experiences been in the distant past? Do they seem disconnected from the present?
2. Does Christian faith shape my values, the way I spend my time, and affect the sources toward which my money flows? Do I see appeals for time and money as intrusions or invitations? Do I resent the poor? Is my life becoming one of increasing generosity?
3. Do I have regular occasions to have fun, to laugh, to smile, to celebrate? When did I last attend or host a party?
4. Do I expect others to serve me, to fulfill my spiritual needs; or do I see myself as a servant? Can I do something for others that is truly anonymous and unselfish? Am I invested in the spiritual growth of one other person?
5. Are the amounts of time and energy that I devote to dieting and fitness in proportion to the amounts of time that I allot for prayer, study, and meditation?
6. Is faith an element of my most important relation-

ships? Is faith essential to some relationships, and
not at all to others? Have I talked about my faith
with those who are closest to me?

7. Have I reflected on the meaning of my own death?
Have I grieved an important loss? Am I able to place
my ultimate trust in God?

Finding a Sanctuary

Of the seven practical suggestions for self-management in Heifetz's *Leadership Without Easy Answers,* this is
by far the briefest (two short paragraphs!). And yet pastors will easily perceive its prominence. The Gospels con-
sistently speak of the importance of finding a sanctuary:
*"In the morning, while it was still very dark, he [Jesus] got
up and went out to a deserted place, and there he prayed"*
(Mark 1:35).

In an earlier chapter I spoke of the importance of holy
times (Sabbath). Now a word about holy places. Use
your imagination for a moment. Can you recall a place
where you felt called, perhaps not with an audible voice
but called nonetheless to a ministry? Some will remember a retreat center or a camp or (literally) a mountaintop.
Others will recall a church sanctuary or an assembly.

Holy places are the settings in which we encounter
God and perceive God's call upon us. They are different:
Moses by the burning bush, Isaiah in the temple, Paul on
the Damascus road, Peter beside the sea of Galilee. My
call to ordained ministry came in the summer between
my junior and senior years in college, at a conference center in western North Carolina. In hindsight I can see that
prevenient grace was at work in my life. I had, after all,
chosen to spend the summer working in a Christian setting; another option had been to test field samples for an
aquatic biology project led by my primary professor in
what was, at the time, my major. At that conference

center the other ways of spending my life seemed, all of a sudden, to be wrong. Where there had been struggle, now there was a peace. Where others had seen gifts, and I had not, a new vision seemed to be emerging. It was the coming together of gift, call, and vocation. And it happened in what became, for me, a sanctuary.

It is not accidental that many men and women discover their gifts on retreats, on Emmaus walks, in extended periods of silence, and in their own holy places. Sanctuaries are "safe places" that allow us to process the gentle movements of the Spirit in our lives. One of the most important sanctuaries in my own journey has been Dayspring, the silent retreat center of the Church of the Saviour in Germantown, Maryland. I have always made my way there with a sense of being buried under the weight of the immediate and the urgent. I have always felt those burdens lifted, just by being in that place. And as the burden of the immediate and the urgent is lifted, I have always reconnected with call and gift. Holy places call forth the contemplative in each of us.

For Reflection: Can you recall a holy place in your life? Can you recall a sanctuary where God was calling forth your gifts?

For Meditation:

A Contemplative

A contemplative is a person
who lives near the temple.
The temple is the place
where miracles happen.

For God's people,
the temple was and is a concrete place
to which men and women would

journey to encounter the holy,
to touch the wall.

For God's people,
the temple is Christ's body,
destroyed and raised again.

And as God's people,
we know that our bodies
are temples of the Holy Spirit.

To be near the temple is to see
the miraculous, the holy.
Miracles happen every day.
The holy is all around us.

The question is not,
"Do I believe in miracles?"
The question is,
"Can I be more aware of the miracles
that are everywhere?"

"What is impossible for you,"
Jesus taught,
"is possible with God."

—K. H. C.

Preserving a Sense of Purpose

Ronald Heifetz offers a final strategy for self-management among leaders in our culture. In doing so he uses the language of meaning, values, and purpose. Someone has noted that at about the same time the church became enamored with the language of management, the business world adopted the language of the church—spirit, mission, gifts. A sense of purpose helps us to remain focused on where we are going. A sense of purpose provides a sense of orientation to the future that God is preparing for us.

In the letter to the Ephesians, Paul uses the imagery of

the body to describe the ideal Christian community. Within the Body of Christ there is a diversity of gifts— apostles, prophets, evangelists, pastors, teachers. The gifts have a purpose: *"to equip the saints for the work of ministry, for building up the body of Christ, until all of us come to the unity of the faith and of the knowledge of the Son of God, to maturity, to the measure of the full stature of Christ"* (Ephesians 4:12-13).

That is a sense of purpose—God has given gifts to each of us, for a purpose. Sometimes we are distracted, sometimes we are discouraged, sometimes we cannot see the forest for the trees—and it helps to be reminded that there is, in the design of God, a sense of purpose about it all. It was never about us, about an individual; it was about a body, a mature, united, growing body of believers who minister to one another and bear witness in the world.

For Reflection and Meditation:

Seven Questions for the Spiritual Journey

1. Do I believe that God has placed unique gifts within me that might be used to help others, and that my primary fulfillment in life will come through the expression of these gifts?
2. Do I believe that I have been created in the image of God, and that my highest goal in life is to reclaim or recover my true identity as a child of God?
3. Do I understand that the implications of questions 1 and 2 lead toward a life of discipline (question 1) and discernment (question 2)?
4. Do I understand that my well-being is linked to the well-being of others, that my salvation, growth, and healing are connected to the salvation, growth, and healing of others, especially those closest to me?

5. Do I understand that my life will be enriched by a willingness to embrace the perspectives of others?
6. Do I recognize that my understanding and expression of the Christian life is but one part of the whole, and that it is in the whole that Jesus Christ is glorified?
7. Do I recognize that I am called to grow in the likeness of Christ, and that my response to God's grace includes a disciplined personal life and a deepening relationship with his Body, the Church?

CHAPTER ELEVEN

A Blessing

Let the peace of Christ rule in your hearts, to
which indeed you were called into the one body.
And be thankful.
(Colossians 3:15)

Dear Ken,
Don't feel completely,
Totally, irrevocably responsible.

That's my job.

Love, God

(note given by a friend and taped to the door
of the closet in my office)

A Guided Meditation

You are tired. You are anxious. There is much to do in this journey, much to accomplish, much to achieve. There are external demands, and there are internal pressures.

One morning you decide, on your way to the office, to take a different route. You drive toward the edge of town and beyond, across a bridge and a little farther. You notice in the distance a narrow dirt road. As you approach that road, you find yourself making the turn and exiting. You follow the road through the brush, which becomes thicker and more lush. After a few miles you discover that you have made it through the thickly covered forest, and you arrive in a clearing.

You step out of your car; and immediately you are greeted by an old friend, a friend you have not seen recently, a friend you have not seen, in fact, in a great while. You make small talk for the long absence in your relationship: There is so much activity, the schedule is already filled, and so on.

You begin to talk, and your friend listens. The pressure, the needs, the expectations, the bottom line: You begin to describe the world in which you live. As you tell the story, your body feels the stress . . . your arms, your shoulders, your head, your chest, your stomach.

Finally, you fall silent. Your friend begins to speak. *"I'm glad that you've come this way today. It has not been accidental. I can appreciate the world in which you live. I do not deny the realities you describe. Allow me simply to invite you to see that world of pressures, of needs, of expectations in a new way. I want to give you a new vision."*

"Let me ask you a question," the friend continues. *"Where do these needs, these expectations, these pressures come from? They do not come from me. I invited you into all of this for a much different purpose. I invited you into my mission. The mission belongs to me—you are not responsible for it—I will take responsibility for the mission. If you have felt that responsibility for all of this as a burden, release it . . . let it go.*

"These people that you serve, they do not belong to you; they also belong to me. They have their own needs, expectations, pressures. You cannot meet their expectations, remove their pressures, satisfy their needs. Neither can you cure, fix, nor save them. Their re-creation is my task. If responsibility for all of them has been a burden to you, release it . . . let it go.

"And while we are talking together, allow me to make one further gentle reminder: You are my child. I have called you, claimed you, engraved you on the palm of my hand. So relax . . . enjoy the beauty that surrounds you, appreciate the friendships that are yours, draw strength from the love that is nearer than you know.

"You belong to me. And if you truly know that, deep within, you will become a steward of my gifts. I have one further word for you, one that you know well, but it is worth repeat-

ing: 'Do not worry about anything, but in everything by prayer and supplication with thanksgiving let your requests be made known to God. And the peace of God, which surpasses all understanding, will guard your hearts and minds in Christ Jesus' " (Philippians 4:6-7).

You embrace your old friend and express gratitude for the words and mostly for the presence. You return to your automobile, settle into it, and make your way, once again, to live and work and pray, reminded that you are a steward of God's gifts, a steward of God's mission, among God's people, in God's world.

Notes

Introduction

1. A Service of Word and Table II, *The United Methodist Hymnal* (Nashville: The United Methodist Publishing House, 1989), p. 10.

1. Spiritual Gifts and You

1. I have been helped by the discussion of Parker Palmer about the loss of our illusions. See *The Active Life* (San Francisco: Harper & Row, 1990), pp. 26ff.

2. On the concept of overfunctioning, or playing the hero, see Edwin Friedman, *Generation to Generation: Family Process in Church and Synagogue* (New York: Guilford Press, 1985), pp. 210ff. and Edwin Friedman, *Friedman's Fables* (New York: Guilford Press, 1990), especially "The Bridge."

3. Max DePree, *Leadership Is an Art* (New York: Doubleday, 1989), p. 7.

4. See *Making Disciples: A New Approach to Confirmation* by William Willimon (Inver Heights, Minn.: Logos, 1990) and *Accompanying the Journey: A Handbook for Sponsors* by Lester Ruth (Nashville: Discipleship Resources, 1997).

5. Eugene Peterson, *Under the Unpredictable Plant: An Exploration in Vocational Holiness* (Grand Rapids, Mich., Eerdmans, 1992), p. 31.

6. "Lessons Learned," *Inc.,* (April, 1995): 35.

7. In *Church Leadership* (Nashville: Abingdon Press, 1993), Lovett Weems outlines the elements of this culture: language, space, symbols, rituals, heroes, and recognitions, daily routines, and cultural network. See chapter 4.

8. Dietrich Bonhoeffer, *Life Together* (New York: Harper & Row, 1954), pp. 97-98.

9. S.H.A.P.E. (Saddleback) and Network (Willow Creek) are discussed in chapter 8 of this book.

10. Churches with multiple staffs should see the composition of these individuals in a similar way. See Brian Bauknight, *Body Building:*

Creating a Ministry Team Through Spiritual Gifts (Nashville: Abingdon Press, 1996).

2. Spiritual Gifts: The Classic Texts from Scripture

1. F. F. Bruce in *The Holy Bible, New Century Version,* copyright © 1987, 1988, 1991 by Word Publishing, Nashville, Tennessee 37214. Used by permission.

2. Richard Hayes, *First Corinthians,* Interpretation: A Bible Commentary for Teaching and Preaching (Louisville: John Knox, 1997), p. 210.

3. Interpretation: *Romans,* p. 197.

4. Philip Kenneson, *Life on the Vine* (Downers Grove, Ill.: Intervarsity Press, 1999), p. 37.

5. For the historical context see 2 Corinthians 8–9.

3. Scripture and Spiritual Gifts: Journaling and Self-Discovery

1. I am grateful to members of Christ United Methodist Church, Greensboro, North Carolina, who participated in this exercise, which formed the basis for my Doctor of Ministry thesis project at Princeton Theological Seminary, entitled "Paradigms of Adult Religious Diversity: Awareness of Christian Vocation by Keeping and Reflecting on a Journal" (1995).

4. Spiritual Gifts: Some Conversation Partners

1. For the concept of "downward mobility," see Henri Nouwen's *Here and Now: Living in the Spirit* (New York: Crossroad, 1995), p. 100. I also commend the classic text, Robert Greenleaf's *Servant Leadership* (New York: Paulist, 1977), pp. 13-14.

2. Peter Block, *Stewardship: Choosing Service over Self-Interest* (San Francisco: Berrett-Koehler, 1993), pp. 9-10.

3. L. Gregory Jones, "The Psychological Captivity of the Church," in *Either/Or* (Grand Rapids, Mich.: Eerdmans, 1995), p. 98.

4. James Bryan Smith, *A Spiritual Formation Workbook* (San Francisco: Harper San Francisco, 1991), p. 44.

5. Brian Wren's hymn text, "Great God, Your Love Has Called Us

Here," copyright © 1977 by Hope Publishing Company, Carol Stream, IL 60188.

6. To learn more about the Disciple Bible Study contact The United Methodist Publishing House at *www.umpublishing.org*. The address of the Dayspring Retreat Center is 11301 Neelsville Church Road, Germantown, Maryland 20876. Among Elizabeth O'Connor's books are *Call to Commitment* (New York: Harper & Row, 1963), which includes the story of the origins of the Dayspring Retreat Center, and *Journey Inward, Journey Outward* (New York: Harper & Row, 1968), which describes the structure and significance of small groups focused around mission.

7. The section on Spiritual Gifts and Stewardship appeared in a revised form in an essay entitled "Money and Ministry," *Circuit Rider* (September 1997). The two works discussed are Richard Foster, *Money, Sex and Power: The Challenge of the Disciplined Life* (San Francisco: Harper & Row, 1985) and Philip Turner, *Sex, Money and Power: An Essay in Christian Social Ethics* (Cambridge: Cowley, 1985).

8. Turner, p. 19.

9. Gordon McDonald, *Ordering Your Private World* (Nashville: Thomas Nelson, 1984), p. 184.

10. For a particularly helpful discussion of this question see Eugene Peterson, *Working the Angles: A Trigonometry for Pastoral Work* (Grand Rapids, Mich.: Eerdmans, 1987).

11. Wayne Oates, *Your Right to Rest* (Philadelphia: Westminster, 1984), p. 29.

12. Walter Brueggemann, *Finally Comes the Poet: Daring Speech for Proclamation* (Minneapolis: Augsburg Fortress, 1989), p. 92.

13. Karl Barth, *Church Dogmatics*, vol. III, *The Doctrine of Creation*, Part Four, (Edinburgh: T&T Clark UK, 1960), p. 54.

14. See Mortimer Arias and Alan Johnson, *The Great Commission: Biblical Models for Evangelism* (Nashville: Abingdon Press, 1992), chapter 1

15. See Gordon Cosby, *By Grace Transformed* (New York: Crossroad, 1999), chapter 11.

16. Edward Sellner, *Mentoring: The Ministry of Spiritual Kinship* (Notre Dame, Ind.: Ave Maria, 1990), p. 61.

5. A Process for Spiritual Gift Identification

1. Danny E. Morris and Charles M. Olsen, *Discerning God's Will Together: A Spiritual Practice for the Church* (Nashville: Upper Room Books, 1997).

2. Ibid., p. 75.

3. Ibid., pp. 78-79.

4. Bonhoeffer, *Life Together,* pp. 97-98.

6. Spiritual Gifts: Some Words of Caution

1. Henri Nouwen, *Life of the Beloved* (New York: Crossroad, 1992), p. 27.

2. Ibid., pp. 27-28.

3. Peter Wagner, *Your Spiritual Gifts Can Help Your Church Grow* (Ventura, Calif.: Regal, 1979), p. 47.

4. For an example of the projection of a particular gift, leadership, see William M. Easum and Thomas Bandy, *Growing Spiritual Redwoods* (Nashville: Abingdon Press, 1997), chapter 7. I am convinced that Bill Easum is an extraordinary leader. And yet it is also true that not every pastor has the gift of leadership.

5. Gilbert G. Bilezikian, *Community 101: Reclaiming the Local Church as a Community of Oneness* (Grand Rapids, Mich.: Zondervan, 1997), p. 97.

6. I am indebted here to the memorial sermon written by William Willimon for one of my mentors, Robert Wilson, a sociologist of religion whose primary interest was the local church and its mission.

7. Teaching Sermons on Spiritual Gifts

1. See John 14. Jesus speaks of the Father dwelling in him and then says "the one who believes in me will also do the works that I do and, in fact, will do greater works than these" (v. 12). This concept is directly related to the sending of the Holy Spirit: "I will ask the Father, and he will give you another Advocate, to be with you forever. This is the Spirit of Truth. . . . I will not leave you orphaned, I am coming to you" (vv. 16-18).

2. Mary Coelho, "Participating in the New Creation," *The Weavings Reader* (Nashville: Upper Room Books, 1993), p. 187.

3. Daniel Iverson, "Spirit of the Living God" (Brentwood, Tenn.: Birdwing Music, © renewal 1963), in *The United Methodist Hymnal,* no. 393.

4. Adelaide A. Pollard, "Have Thine Own Way, Lord," in *The United Methodist Hymnal,* no. 382.

5. Gerald May, *Addiction and Grace* (San Francisco: Harper & Row, 1988), p. 17.

6. Elizabeth O'Connor, *The Eighth Day of Creation* (Waco: Word, 1971). The title is taken from the Christian philosopher Nicholas

Berdayaev, "Creativeness in the world is, as it were, the eighth day of creation."

7. Mark 1:11. Compare carefully with Matthew 3:17.

8. Cosby, *Mission Groups*, p. 47.

9. Gordon Fee, *Paul, the Spirit and the People of God* (Peabody, Maine: Hendrickson, 1996), p. 63.

10. Ibid., p. 72.

11. O'Connor, *Eighth Day*, p. 13.

12. From Martin Buber, *The Way of Man* (New York: Carol Publishing, 1985).

13. Bonhoeffer, *Life Together*, p. 20.

14. Jim Jackson, "Comparisons," *Spiritual Lessons from Life* (May 17, 1996).

15. See Richard Bolles, *The Three Boxes of Life: And How to Get Out of Them* (Berkeley: Ten Speed Press, 1981), p. 14.

16. From Anne Lamott, *Bird by Bird: Some Instructions on Writing and Life* (New York: Pantheon, 1994), p. 167.

17. Henri Nouwen, *The Inner Voice of Love: A Journey Through Anguish to Freedom* (New York: Doubleday, 1996), pp. 21-22.

9. The Journey Toward Our Spiritual Gifts

1. For an insightful and hilarious account of spirituality, the gifts of pastoring and administration and new church development, see Eugene Peterson, *Under the Unpredictable Plant* (Grand Rapids, Mich.: Eerdmans, 1992).

2. Michael Mott, *The Seven Mountains of Thomas Merton* (San Diego: Harcourt Brace, 1984).

3. Thomas Merton, *The Wisdom of the Desert* (Search Press Ltd. [UK], 1996), p. 22.

4. Thomas Merton, *Thoughts in Solitude* (Boston: Shambhala, 1993), p. 89.

5. Patrick Hart, ed., *Thomas Merton, Monk* (Kalamazoo, Mich.: Cistercian Publications, 1974), p. 80.

6. Thomas Merton, *The Sign of Jonas* (San Diego: HarBrace Harvest Books, 1979), p. 22.

7. James Finley, *Merton's Palace of Nowhere* (Notre Dame, Ind.: Ave Maria, 1978), p. 38.

8. I find the work of Henri Nouwen in *Life of the Beloved* to echo this point of Merton's.

9. Thomas Merton, *New Seeds of Contemplation* (New York: Directions, 1972), p. 31.

10. Merton, *Jonas,* p. 32.

11. Neill Q. Hamilton, *Maturing in the Christian Life: A Pastor's Guide* (Philadelphia: Geneva, 1984), pp. 68-69.

12. Merton, *Jonas,* p. 89.

13. Merton, *Jonas,* p. 334.

10. A Sending Forth:
Spiritual Gifts Without Easy Answers

1. See Fee, *Paul,* pp. 5ff.

2. Richard Heifetz, *Leadership Without Easy Answers* (Cambridge: Harvard University Press, 1994).

3. See Gilbert Meilaender, *Friendship: A Study in Theological Ethics* (Notre Dame, Ind.: University of Notre Dame Press, 1985), chapter 5.

4. See Richard Foster's explanation in *Prayer: Finding the Heart's True Home* (San Francisco: Harper San Francisco, 1992), chapter 3.

5. Craig Dykstra, *Vision and Character: A Christian Educator's Alternative to Kohlberg* (Mahwah, N.J.: Paulist Press, 1981), p. 103.